Parents and Digital Technology

Children today are digital natives, growing up in an age where social media and online communication is the norm. This book is an indispensable guide for parents who may feel they are struggling to keep up, addressing the issues that young people and their families face in the world of modern technology. Suzie Hayman, a parenting counsellor, and John Coleman, a distinguished psychologist, use their combined expertise to explore the challenges and possibilities of being constantly connected, helping parents to make choices about how they communicate, set boundaries and establish rules.

Using real-world examples and solid psychological theory, the book looks first at the anxieties parents express about digital technology, followed by the serious potential threats such as cyber-bullying, sexting and easy access to pornographic or violent materials. However, the internet is also full of enormous potential and a further chapter explores the positive side of the digital playground. The authors also share their expert understanding of child and adolescent development and how this relates to the appeal of digital media, with special attention paid to the importance of good communication. The end result is a toolbox for parents, full of tips, strategies and techniques designed to help navigate the digital world, ensuring it is safe yet still exciting for young people.

Parents and Digital Technology is essential reading for all parents and guardians, as well as those caring for children and teenagers in a professional setting, who want to get the best out of life and modern technology while keeping safe in a family that talks to each other, spends time with each other and enjoys each other.

Suzie Hayman is a Relate-trained counsellor, an accredited parenting educator, an agony aunt and the author of 30 books on parenting.

John Coleman is a psychologist whose primary interest is adolescence. His pioneering work with parents and families has been widely recognised, and in 2001 he was awarded an OBE for his services to young people.

Parents and Digital Technology:
How to raise the connected generation

*Suzie Hayman and
John Coleman*

Routledge
Taylor & Francis Group

LONDON AND NEW YORK

First published 2016
by Routledge
2 Park Square, Milton Park, Abingdon, Oxon OX14 4RN

and by Routledge
711 Third Avenue, New York, NY 10017

Routledge is an imprint of the Taylor & Francis Group, an informa business

© 2016 Suzie Hayman and John Coleman

The right of Suzie Hayman and John Coleman to be identified as authors of this work has been asserted by them in accordance with sections 77 and 78 of the Copyright, Designs and Patents Act 1988.

British Library Cataloguing in Publication Data

A catalogue record for this book is available from the British Library

Library of Congress Cataloging-in-Publication Data

A catalog record for this book has been requested

ISBN: 978-1-138-93315-6 (hbk)
ISBN: 978-1-138-93316-3 (pbk)
ISBN: 978-1-315-67870-2 (ebk)

Typeset in New Century Schoolbook
by Apex CoVantage, LLC

Contents

Acknowledgements

We are grateful to many people for their advice whilst we were working on this project. We acknowledge the help of our colleagues at Family Lives, the Association for Young People's Health, and the Who Cares Trust. We would like to thank all those parents and young people who we have quoted in this book. They kindly agreed to be interviewed, and allowed us to use their experiences to inform our thinking. Our own families have played an important role, especially the younger generation. We thank our sons and daughters, grandchildren and stepchildren for helping us to understand what it is like growing up with the internet and with the digital devices that are part of life today. Finally a special thanks to our partners, Vic and Jenny, who have provided encouragement and support during our collaboration in the writing of this book.

Suzie and John

Introduction

"If you have a child, you'll notice they have two states;
asleep or online."

Eric Schmidt, Chair of Google

"I hardly see my son these days, he's on his mobile phone
or tablet from the time he leaves school to when he
goes to bed – and often beyond that! I know I check my
Facebook page all too often but I'm just lost at how I can
get him to talk to me. Trying to get him to put it all aside
to come and be with us just leads to arguments. I have no
idea what he does all that time."

Letter to Suzie Hayman's *Woman*
magazine agony page

"Our sires' age was worse than our grandsires'. We, their
sons, are more worthless than they; so in our turn we
shall give the world a progeny yet more corrupt."

Horace, Book III of *Odes*, circa 20 BC

In 2015 TV Channel 4 broadcast a series about teenage life in
which they followed 13 sixth formers for nine months, tracking every tweet, WhatsApp, Facebook and Instagram post
they exchanged. It amounted to over a million exchanges.

Being a parent has never been easy. We have often felt
challenged by our young charges – you can find quotes from
parents and other adults bemoaning the bad manners and
careless behaviour of children and teenagers from Socrates'

Athens to Shakespeare's London, and beyond. Psychologist and educator Granville Stanley Hall said:

> "Never has youth been exposed to such dangers of both perversion and arrest as in our own land and day. Increasing urban life with its temptations, prematurities, sedentary occupations, and passive stimuli just when an active life is most needed, early emancipation and a lessening sense for both duty and discipline, the haste to know and do all befitting man's estate before its time, the mad rush for sudden wealth and the reckless fashions set by its gilded youth – all these lack some of the regulatives they still have in older lands with more conservative conditions."

Apart from some of the words used, doesn't that sound like the sort of complaint we hear so often these days? He said this in 1904 in his book *The Psychology of Adolescence*.

In many ways, the job of parent has hardly changed since we climbed from the primordial ooze. We worry about outside influences, our skills, our children's abilities or their demands, and always have done. And yet, a wholly new issue with wholly new consequences appears to have developed in the last 25 years – digital technology and the internet. Should we worry about it, and our children's use of it, or celebrate it? Should we try to control their use or leave them to it? And is it really that different to the sorts of opportunities or indeed dangers we encountered when we were young?

Many of our children are 'digital natives'. By this we mean they were all born into and grew up in this world. Most of them know the language, are comfortable with using the technology, feel happy to manipulate and even make the customs. They have little fear about simply diving in and having a go. Depending on what access they have to the technology at home or at school, they may be proficient in coding or simply able to use texting and social media. To them it is merely a resource to be used, a playground to access as much as they can.

Some parents – particularly those with young children – may be equally at home and nonchalant about the possibilities and the potential. Tablets and smart phones, apps and social media are part of their lives and aspects they take for granted. They use it all, so why shouldn't their children? But some parents are better described as digital immigrants, coming into new territory and perhaps struggling with the language and customs found there. Immigrants to the digital world can range from those who have dipped their toes into the digital world, to those who have moved on from sending texts on their mobiles and emails on their laptops to using social media, to those who have so integrated into the village that they feel fully at home. And they are occasionally brought up short when a 'local' reminds them they are 'recent arrivals'! The reality is that for most parents our children, even those of primary school age, probably know a lot more about digital media than we do.

They seem so much more at home in this field, and we often feel at a loss about what they might be doing. For this reason many parents say knowing how to deal with digital media is No. 1 on their list of anxieties. That lack of knowledge, or lack of confidence in what knowledge we have, results in our finding it difficult to know what to say and how to discuss this issue. That's true whether it's with our children or with the other adults we know, such as relatives, friends or our children's teachers. And even those with total facility, who perhaps have brought children into the world to be surrounded by digital technology and parents who use it all the time, are beginning to wonder whether simply accepting what is offered to us online is the best approach. Should we be considering how we and our children use digital technology and the internet? Should we be having discussions with them about all our use? Is there a need for boundaries and rules?

In this book we (John Coleman – a distinguished Oxford University psychologist whose primary focus is adolescence – and Suzie Hayman – a counsellor, agony aunt, accredited parenting educator and author) will address the issues surrounding what young people and their parents face, now and in the future. We'll explore what both the challenges and the possibilities might be and will provide tips, strategies and techniques to help parents make choices about how they communicate, set boundaries and establish rules. We hope that the end result will be to help parents and young people to get the best out of life and modern technology while keeping safe in a family that talks to each other, spends time with each other and enjoys each other. This is a manifesto for understanding and being in control; for managing our and our children's use and balancing the advantages and disadvantages of what we and they may be encountering.

What will we offer to help you make sense of what your children are doing and why, and what you can and perhaps should be doing about it? We'll look first at the anxieties parents express about internet and digital technology. We'll be using real-world evidence: the results from discussion with parents and young people, and letters and emails from them, surveys and data from charities that help parents with such issues. The words, queries and ideas from parents and young people will feature throughout the book. You may find your anxieties echoed by other parents – you may uncover a few that haven't yet occurred to you, or realise you have some that don't feature here. We'll then look at the actual worries we think you should have, and follow with the more serious threats, which may reassure you or focus your mind on what needs to be done. On a more upbeat note, we'll then explore the positives in the digital world, which is likely both to inspire and restore confidence in what is out there for you and your children.

We will then take a look at child and adolescent development. We as parents cannot understand the digital world our children inhabit, and learn how to respond to it, unless we also understand something about the way our children develop and how this reflects on their internet use, and the appeal of digital media. You don't need to be a university psychologist or a counsellor to understand your child – it just helps to have one of each offering you some insight to help you do so! We'll offer assistance on effective, positive parenting. Setting boundaries around internet and digital use starts with being able to confidently set boundaries around other behaviour, and understand why such boundaries are important.

We'll explore communication – how to listen as much as talk, how to phrase questions and how to open channels of communication, and how to dive under bad behaviour to understand what is really going on. We'll explore our own use of and understanding of digital media, and how this impacts on our ability or desire to help our children. We'll look at how to guide them, discipline them and ultimately, once we have reason to trust them, have confidence in them doing their best for themselves. And we'll look at the particular issues families living apart from each other may experience in this area and what to do about them. These may be families in which parents have separated or children are fostered or adopted or living with members of their family other than their parents – kinship care.

In effect, this book will be a toolbox, designed to help you navigate the digital world and make it both safe and still exciting for yourselves and your children.

Why are any of us but perhaps especially young people and children so drawn to digital technology? One reason may be that shiny toys, whether real or online, are appealing to us all. Gaming is fun. Talking to friends is fun. For young people, being different or having separate realms from adults is fun. Being better – more skilled – than adults is even more fun. Children want to imitate their parents – so if you use digital tech, they will want to too. They also eventually want to go one better. All these draw young people to screens.

But what we as adults perhaps less knowledgeable and skilled in these fields need to accept is – why wouldn't they? Digital technology has made so many new activities available to all of us, with young people in the vanguard. Some of us might have been able to make music, write novels, take and edit photographs in the past. Now all of us can do so, and so easily. And much, much more. No wonder they gravitate towards the internet and its possibilities.

Commercial interests, keen to take advantage of all this, make their products available in ways and under certain conditions that harness all of our love of the new and exciting. And, often, of the free – or what looks to be free. Adults, however, may be able to recognise that if it seems too good to be true it possibly is, and to be more cynical and careful about online behaviour. Children, with their naiveté, and teenagers, with their inherent love of excitement and risk, can put themselves in undesirable situations.

Many of the challenges families face in the digital world are hardly new. Bullying has always occurred, young people have always grasped at excuses not to do homework or chores or even join in with the rest of the family, and teenagers have always got hold of pornography. None are new threats because of digital media. But certain aspects of these issues have changed with digital use, and we all need to understand and know how to deal with this development.

Our aim is to explore digital technology and internet use, and help you work out how you and your family may best make use of what is enormous potential. But equally, to keep yourself and your family safe from what can be problematical. If you are concerned, we hope to reassure you that you are not the only ones experiencing worry and difficulties with this issue. We're confident that whatever fears or conflict you may be having at the moment, letting us help and guide you can make a difference. We hope to help you gain the confidence and skills to make a difference in your family.

What can you do online?

One of the comments made repeatedly by parents we spoke to when researching and writing this book, even those with regular use themselves, was "What do they do on there?" Sometimes it was in exasperation, as in "What on earth do they find to spend so much time looking and tapping on those machines?" At other times it was genuine puzzlement, confusion and wonder as in "I really don't understand the world they are accessing." So before we go any further it is important to consider what young people (and you, in fact) can do and often choose to do on computers or devices. On the whole, we're going to try to be sparing in naming particular websites, games, and applications purely because these change and develop so quickly – what is a favourite and 'must use' for our youngsters today will be used by parents tomorrow and old hat by next week. We will name some as examples – forgive us if they've already gone out of favour!

But most of what you and your children can do fits into one or other or several of the following categories.

This is what people seek to do with digital devices:

Connect: be in touch with their face-to-face friends; be in touch with family; be in touch with people they see as friends but have never met; be in touch with random strangers; be in touch with a wider community.

Connect using: texts, messages, pictures, pre-filmed videos or live video calls via Facetime, Skype or Google Hangout, posts on social media sites. Accessing these via computers, phones, Blackberry Messenger, games consoles and other handheld or home-based devices. Information can be passed on through text-based messages, spoken word, videos with or without sound and emojis (little ideograms or pictures that convey emotion – a smile, a wink, a tear).

Talk anonymously: sites – forums and message boards – such as Yik Yak and Secret allow users to post anonymously with comments and questions – Ask.fm allows you the choice to show a name or be anonymous. Some sites are geofenced – that is, only allow you to be in contact with people near you. Or they use your own and other users' contacts lists so that you are only in contact with people you know or who are known by people you know, albeit anonymously.

Find out stuff: use search engines such as Google and Bing to research and learn, for school/education, to research and learn for personal interest or to answer anxieties (about sex, health, weight, etc.) or go WWILFing (What Was I Looking For) – simply following links from one website you were on for a reason to another and then another, turning up all sorts of bits of information for the fun of it. Or follow links and look for websites suggested by friends or seen in the media.

Play games: play games alone; play games with friends; play online with friends; play online with other users; using websites, apps or games downloaded or on DVDs; on computers, laptops, tablets, phones or games consoles.

Be entertained: view films, TV programmes, videos, pictures on sites such as YouTube, WhatsApp, Instagram etc. Read books and other text content, on computers or reading devices such as Kindle. Listen to radio programmes.

Shop: using online shops or online facilities offered by real-world shops to buy toys, games, DVDs, clothing etc. etc. Also, to buy virtual or online items or add-ons for games, particularly multiplayer online role-playing games. With gift cards or vouchers or their parents' credit or debit cards, with or without permission.

Music: stream music (ie play in real time on a website), download music (ie transfer music to your own device to play when you want when not on the internet) for free or paid; learn how to play a musical instrument, compose and make music and upload for friends or the wider community to enjoy.

Make content: take photos, write – either 'diary entries' (blogging), or short stories, novels, factual writing, plays or screenplays – make short or long videos (vlogging), make films, create animations or comics or graphic novels; do any or all of these for yourself, your friends and family, the world at large.

Send content: send texts, messages, pictures, sound files and videos to people you know.

Upload content: put videos on sites such as Vine or YouTube; photos, drawings, text and videos on sites such as Snapchat; texts, photos, audio and videos on sites such as WhatsApp; photos on sites such as Instagram. On some sites or apps you can keep the content private for the people you choose to invite to view, on others you can make them public. You should access and regularly check and update your privacy settings. You can't always trust, however, private will remain private. Snapchat's selling point was that users could send content to a controlled list of recipients – or one recipient – and set the amount of time before the content would delete itself. However, users found ways of saving snaps and then mailing these to other friends and an app was quickly developed that did this for you.

Chat with people you know: online chatrooms or social media sites allow you to chat (in text) with friends in real time.

Chat with people you don't know: sites such as Omegle allow you to chat anonymously online with another user. You can accept the site's random pick, or add your interests so the site can find someone interested in the same things.

Take and share photos: this comes into so many of the other elements – making content, connecting – but the sheer ease with which people with digital tech can make and share pictures makes this one of the most used facilities. You can take photos on a mobile phone or tablet and share with your friends/contacts directly or via Facebook, Instagram, WhatsApp, Flikr, Dropbox and many others. Person to person means only they see the photo in the first instance although of course they can then share it as they choose. Depending on the privacy settings you apply, uploading via an app or tablet to an online site means pictures can be seen only by people you invite, a wider audience or the whole world.

Make a difference: joining in conversations on open sites such as Twitter allows people to have their voice heard. One person objecting, demanding change, highlighting what they see as injustice does little. Thousands doing so can be effective. Online petitions do lead to change, such as the request that Sir Nicolas Winton, who saved children from the Nazis, be honoured in a Royal Mail stamp. Viral campaigns such as the Ice Bucket Challenge can raise awareness, and charitable funds.

Meet people: sites such as Tinder allow you to upload details and then ask you to scroll through other users' details, usually within a specified location, to see if there are other people you might like. If you select someone and they select you too, the site puts you in touch. You can chat through the app, or arrange to meet – you will be nearby.

Do sex: find and view pornography and watch it or masturbate to it; use webcams or mobile phones to film yourself or other people in sexual poses or acts and ask for or take part in sexual activity. See above – Blendr (straight relationships) and Grindr (gay relationships) are far more sex oriented than Tinder where dates can be platonic; Blendr or Grindr dates tend not to be!

Create an online presence: have a blog (as a day-to-day diary of your life, or as things you want to say) or do the same via videos, called vlogs, and have a channel on a site such as YouTube (that is, an area where you place all your videos). Make it public so people will learn about you.

Monetise your online presence: have sufficient followers to allow you to charge for advertisements, or be paid to mention or show yourself using brand objects. Successful vloggers have gone on to launch their own beauty or clothing products and publish books. Or, indeed, charge users to see, and ask you to act out their choice of, sexual activity.

Something for you to try

Ask yourself – which of these do you do? And which do your offspring do? Make a list and compare with your children. Would you like to do any of these? Are there any aspects of digital use we haven't covered?

Take the opportunity to talk it through with your family – ask for their advice and guidance. Get them to take you through the uses they have heard about. It's always better to request help than to interrogate. Asking for their thoughts and ideas will always work better than appearing to act as the police!

2

What parents tell us about their worries

The internet has been with us for a quarter of a century. During that time digital devices have become infinitely more sophisticated and of course more accessible in all sorts of ways – cheaper, smaller, more user friendly. Parents today might have grown up with digital technology in its development but be neither heavy users nor entirely comfortable with new technology. Others use regularly but remember a time when it was still all new. And some embrace and feel at home on all forms of digital device. Using digital devices yourself, however, may not mean you feel comfortable about how your children may be managing a digital world.

There is no doubt that many parents have significant anxieties about their children's use of the internet, social media and digital technology. We communicated with a variety of people, took views from letters to Suzie's agony page, and from the family charity for which we are both trustees, Family Lives, which has over a million contacts with parents every year. From all of these sources we know that there are certain issues that seem to worry most people. So let's consider what are the concerns most frequently voiced by parents.

Access to pornography and violence

"What are they accessing online? You hear so many scare stories about porn and other difficult content. Scares the life out of me!"

Sally, parent of 12-year-old boy and 14-year-old girl

Most parents know that pornography is freely available and accessible on the internet. Some, of course, view it themselves – not always with honest communication between couples about their use. Whether they see it themselves or not, many do worry their children may be viewing inappropriate material – explicit pictures or videos of sexual activity.

> "I've always felt it was our job to tell our children about sex although I am relieved schools are taking more of a role than they did when I was a pupil – my sex ed was rubbish. But I must admit I've left it till I felt he was ready and now I've had people tell me it's 'shutting the barn door after the horse has bolted' time – at his age he's bound to have heard far too much already. He has said he's not interested in girls, he's into football but I'm not at all sure that's as reassuring as I'd like it to be."
>
> Tom, father of an 11-year-old son

Certainly, parents who expressed this anxiety were aware that if their children were accessing pornography online, they may be the last to know.

Violence was another concern – parents felt some television programmes went too far even before the watershed of 9pm, and that it wasn't always possible to police their children's viewing habits after that time. Violence in games was also mentioned but, although some parents gamed themselves and some played with their children, a significant number we heard from admitted to be utterly baffled by digital media games and not to have accessed them themselves.

There was much confusion over how young people might hear about pornography. Even parents who had accessed or did use pornography themselves felt their children would hear about it through friends or acquaintances, or while on the internet. But they questioned how – would they have been searching for it? And how would you prevent that happening?

Having the technical know-how to exercise control

"I recently found out that as soon as I put parental blocks
on our computer he dismantles them – he knows far
more about it than I do."

Letter to Suzie from parent with 13-year-old son

Parents on the whole were aware you could put blocking programs in place, or ask your internet provider to put such a
service in place. Most felt it was either too difficult or futile
as young people tend to be better at removing blocks than
parents are at applying them. And blocks applied at source
by providers then affected content adults might want to see.
What to use, whether to use, how to use were all anxieties
felt by many parents.

One of the downsides of using a blocking program is
that apart from giving you false security it can also block
sites that have explicit content, but for legitimate reasons.
These may be sites a young person may be using for school
research, or sites someone worrying about sex or sexuality
and wanting perfectly reasonable answers that school or
home are not providing or that they feel inhibited about asking, might seek out.

Extra on the bills

"A friend of mine said her children had been able to
run up enormous bills without her being able to stop
it. That just horrifies me!"

Tamsin, mother of a 7-year-old son
and 12-year-old daughter

Unintended costs are also a concern. Until it happened
to them, many parents had no idea they could find themselves liable for large bills run up by even young children
on new tablets. Parents now do know and worry, but often
have no idea how to stop it. Some games and apps running
on tablets and mobile phones or indeed on some laptops
regularly offer upgrades and extras that can be bought

with just a tap, charging automatically to the person who bought the device, often with little delay or warning, unless they've configured it otherwise. Most retailers now offer to block such access or set it up so that you have to tap in a password each time but parents worry that it might not be enough to protect them.

Downloading viruses

"We kept getting problems with our computer and a friend would come over and get it back working again, finding all sorts of viruses and stuff. We were really strict about clicking on emails so we couldn't understand where they were coming from. It wasn't until we finally took it in to the shop that they asked if we had children – yes – if they ever brought home DVDs from friends – yes – and if we had virus protection that alerted us to websites that could be harmful and if so, did we take notice? Well, we would but I wasn't so sure our kids did. And sure enough, that's where all the trouble was coming from."

Sally, parent of 12-year-old boy and 14-year-old girl

Many parents worried about and had experienced problems with often costly damage to computers through viruses. Most knew to be careful, and teach their children to be careful, about clicking on links in emails. However, there was some confusion expressed about how else viruses could get access and how that could be prevented.

The age at which you might need to consider your children need protection

"I do worry but then mine are 7 and 9 so I think we've got a few years before we have to do anything"

Geoff, father to two boys

Many parents have anxieties, but do feel they have some leeway before they have to take measures to protect young children from what might be out there. The assumption often seems to be that it's teenagers who might seek out or be offered porn not primary school pupils and that young children won't be seeing games or films that depict sex or violence.

The age of your child or children may influence how secure or threatened you feel about their digital use. Too young, and you may – incorrectly – feel they are not yet at risk. Older and you may – again, incorrectly – feel they are out of control and there is nothing you can do. Whatever your children's ages, you need to consider a family digital strategy.

Selfies and sexting

"I'm sure we were never this vain – or what is it? I suppose the difference is that when I was young taking a picture involved film and processing and expense. They just click on their phones. But it can't be healthy!"

Wendy, mother of daughters aged 14 and 16

Most parents know about selfies – the almost relentless drive that so many young people (and many adults!) seem to have acquired to document their life through photos taken on their mobile phones. One worry for parents is that it does seem to fuel anxiety and confusion. Young people post the results on social media and then agonise if the pictures are not liked or approved by their peers, but despair if they are accepted because it means they have to keep up the standard. The poses used are often seen by parents as inappropriate – said Wendy, "They all seem to do this awful starlet thing with pouted lips, looking sidelong at the lens with hair all over their faces."

The other aspect that worries some parents is the possibility their daughters may be involved in sexting. This involves girls being asked to provide pictures of themselves in as sexual a manner as possible – scantily clad, topless, fully naked. Parents have heard that many boys ask for such pictures as a preliminary to asking a girl out on a date – show me, and then I'll ask you out (if you pass muster). It can also involve boys sending pictures of themselves in poses meant to show off muscular arms, abs or chests; or indeed, their genitals.

In a private conversation, 15-year-old Beth told her mother and Suzie that she and her friends are regularly asked by boys at her school to send them topless 'selfies'. She refuses and is most scathing about those who do so. She says the boys rarely keep their promises that the picture would be 'for their eyes only' and most are either circulated round school or even put on the internet. She also says the pressure to join in and be like all the rest comes from other girls, not from the boys who respect her resistance. But she also says it has cost her friends and has led to unpleasant texts and postings online.

Body image

Parents often despair at what seems to be a widespread obsession among young people to have 'the right body'. What can be frightening are the unrealistic standards – girls supposed to have big breasts but minuscule waists and even young teenage boys aspiring to muscles that would take hours daily in a gym and/or steroids to acquire. Parents may battle with youngsters who avoid healthy food yet will snack on junk food because it seems easier to maintain an idea of 'dieting' that way. Children as young as 8 or 9 or younger may begin to refuse certain foods, worry about their diet and image, and be stressed and even depressed about it. It's not simply a matter of weight – children and young people may begin to express the fear that they do not 'look right'. Lack of self-confidence and self-esteem can then effect their education, their friendships and their family relationships.

Cyberbullying

One of the concerns quite frequently expressed is about cyberbullying, where young people are harassed online or through texts and messages by people they know or by strangers. In an online survey the family charity Family Lives found 43% of 11- to 16-year-olds had been bullied on social networks such as Facebook, Twitter, Bebo and Myspace. (The popularity of the last two has all but collapsed.) The site Ask.fm has caused particular concern after being linked to several teenage suicides. Ask.fm had around 180 million monthly users, 40% of which are younger than 18 and allowed posters to remain anonymous. However, although bullying remains a major worry for parents they tend to focus on real-world harassment, and are less aware of what happens in the cyber world. This may be because, as young people say, it is easier to hide and easier to get away with online bullying than face-to-face harassment.

Communication and family cohesion

"I never see my teenage son. I struggle to communicate with any of my children. All three have televisions and laptops in their rooms, and seem to spend all their time there. We seldom eat together as a family. I maintain a fridge and a freezer full of meals and they tend to be taken when each person chooses because I can never get them to come to the table together and they never agree on what they want – and won't eat if it's something they don't like."

Sara, mother of 17- and 11-year-old sons
and a 14-year-old daughter

One of the big issues that many parents worry about is the way that social media and the internet have taken over family life. They say constant media use has destroyed family time. It may seem as if you are recalling a mythical Golden Age to hark back to the days when "We made our own entertainment, gathering round to play games, talk, sing in the evening because there was little else to do." But it's not that unrealistic to recall a time when it was common to eat an evening meal as a family and then, again as a family, settle down in a room to watch television together. With corresponding and sometimes bitter arguments over what to watch, which was why cheaper televisions and other devices allowing people to go to separate rooms if they disagreed seemed a boon. Families are now realising the downside – that families may share time together less and less and the lack of acrimony is matched by a lack of connection and cohesion.

Distraction

"We've had arguments when I'm speaking and she's got her head in her phone. There has been plenty of talk about the rudeness and disrespect of doing this in front of others. It still happens sometimes. I feel this happens with most kids her age or around us."

> Ben, father of 13-year-old son and
> 16-year-old daughter

Many parents worry about the way their children seem to simply tune out much of the time – their attention is on their device rather than what is happening in the room, especially at what should be 'family time'. Said Carla, who has daughters aged 12, 14 and 16: "I got so fed up with trying to talk with my children over the evening meal, while they are either blatantly texting or doing it under the table, I told them I was going to confiscate their phones if they didn't stop. My eldest daughter told me in all seriousness that she would rather die than hand hers over."

Parents report feeling not only anxious about this but about their perceived helplessness – that they feel they have no way of calling a halt and stopping it.

And it's not just other people at home from whom they disengage. Said Carla, "I've noticed that kids hanging out together will still be texting people who aren't there. Sometimes you see a group of them and not one is actually talking to anyone there, they're ignoring those present and texting or messaging or whatever. Are they learning to socialise with real people?"

Life, but not as we know it . . .

"My concern is that time spent on social media is time not spent on other real-life activities. We used to go out as a family, cycle or walk together. And at home we'd cook together – make cakes and things. All of that has gone by the board – they do no outdoor pursuits at all, and they used to enjoy it."

> Carla, who has daughters aged 12, 14 and 16

Parents expressed sadness at no longer sharing certain activities with their children. But they also had considerable unease at the fact that their children no longer seemed to want to engage in any fitness or outdoor activity on their own or with friends. There were concerns at the health issues of long periods spent on devices – little exercise, no fresh air, increased consumption of unhealthy snacks and junk food. "All she seems to want when she's spent hours on that machine is biscuits and coke," said Timna, who has a 15-year-old daughter.

That it takes up too much time

"I've always known what mine does online and what they do or are seeing doesn't really worry me. It's mostly Facebook, chatting with friends and studying. I'm okay with it except the amount. Too much, far too much."

Gina, mother of 12-year-old daughter
and 17-year-old son

Parents express concern at how much time their children spend on their devices but also admit to bafflement at how to either contain or monitor it. Says Saul, with sons aged 8 and 12 and a daughter aged 15, "How much time is too much? And can we as 40-somethings really understand their world in this sense? When I question it they tell me all their friends are on for much longer than they are. Hard to believe but it does seem true!" But parents often despair at what they see of as a waste of time that they feel could be spent doing more worthwhile activities in the real world.

Drawing the line

"It's hard to find the line between trust and supervision – I checked our 14-year-old girl's Facebook and discovered she was online as 17."

Wendy, with 14- and 16-year-old daughters

Parents frequently struggle with knowing when to intervene, when to stand back, when to be suspicious and when to trust. Some felt they got it right only to discover their children had overstepped a mark behind their backs, leaving them feeling betrayed. Others felt that being over cautious had damaged trust and made dealing with the issues more difficult.

Parental consistency

"I know I swing wildly from one week to the next on what I'll allow and what I'll clamp down on. I'll hear about something awful and just about ban them from any use for days, then let them back and leave them to it. I know that's not ideal."

   Ben, father of 13-year-old son and 16-year-old daughter

Parents fear the result of the perfect storm – secrecy and defensiveness on the part of their child meeting ignorance or confusion or lack of engagement from a parent. It's common for parents to swing from being tough to being laid-back, realising neither is an effective way of dealing with the situation and that being inconsistent is itself destructive.

How you deal with your children's digital use can be a touchstone for how you can deploy your parenting skills. Children need communication, boundaries, firm but fair rules. If you feel you're not applying these to their digital use, we will be offering some guidance on strategies that can help.

Education, education, education

"I really worry about the way 'text speak' is dumbing down – how does it impact their ability to spell and express themselves clearly for school, university and later in jobs? And the way they flit about from one thing to another, will they ever learn to knuckle down and do anything in depth?"

Sara, mother of 17- and 11-year-old sons
and a 14-year-old daughter

In spite of digital devices now being integrated into teaching in many schools, a common theme for many parents was the way they felt digital use, especially messaging, posting and texting, was unhelpful. Short, brief messages, especially on platforms such as Twitter that limit users to 140 characters, encourage young people to ignore spelling, grammar, traditional forms of address, and parents did find this alarming with a view to whether they would be able to adapt when more 'correct' forms were needed, in school, exams and the workplace.

That they pay more attention to friends than you

Parents of young people, particularly of teenagers, have always felt in competition with their children's friends. Do they pay more attention to what their friends think, believe or say than they do to you? Are you valued and listened to as much as the best friend? This might have felt difficult when young people came home full of what so-and-so said, thought or did at school today or what they might have shared when together. It feels that much more acute when those friends seem to have entry into your home and your child's bedroom, and certainly their attention, 24/7.

Not knowing what they're up to

"They spend a lot of time on their phones, even when they're in physical company with their friends. I really do wonder what on earth they're getting up to and every time I try to read up on it, it baffles me."

Paul, father of 9-year-old son and 13- and
15-year-old daughters

Parents worry about not understanding the world their children take for granted – the applications they use or indeed the way they relate to each other via social media. Parents have always felt excluded to a certain extent from part of their children's lives. Children encourage this by use of things such a slang – a private language that constantly evolves and changes so that users can keep up and understand each other, non-users cannot. Social media and digital technology seem to have a similar advantage – useful to employ and having the additional reward of delineating who's in and who's out.

That you don't understand so are losing control

"It really upsets me that I have no idea what my children do with their phones. My two daughters seem to spend so much time giggling and comparing stuff on their phones and my son sits there all aloof and superior. I can't get them to listen to any rules or boundaries because I simply don't know what they do!"

Hannah, mother of 15-year-old daughter
and stepdaughter, and 17-year-old son

Parents have always found it hard to let go and both recognise and accept that their children are beginning to stand on their own two feet. One common anxiety about digital technology is that, because it can baffle us and the way our young people use it may seem beyond us, we feel upset and resent the loss of control this implies. Even younger parents who are regular users can still feel one or several steps behind their children.

Your own digital use and whether it contributes to the problem

"OK, I'm writing this and as I do so I can see it's a problem. But the truth is the first thing my husband and I do when arriving home is to check emails, texts and social media. I'll do it as I walk in the door on my phone, my husband is doing it on his walk from the station. Our kids do it on the bus and they keep on doing it throughout the evening. So do we – I have my tablet on in the kitchen while I'm making dinner and he's on his phone in the living room."

Sara, mother of 17- and 11-year-old sons
and a 14-year-old daughter

Many parents worry about the example they give their children on digital technology use. Some parents do both work as well as personal email on home-based devices, some use mobile phones. Some use Facebook and Twitter, others use those and other social media. Whether you are a newbie or an early adopter, a regular or a light user you may be concerned that your own behaviour carries with it powerful messages about what is or is not acceptable. Parents told us they felt they needed rules about use at home but were not sure what to say, when to say it or how to promote them.

The main issues

These are the issues felt by many parents to be the main anxieties they have about their children's use of digital technology. You may agree – you may have other or additional concerns. But are there more issues, and more dangerous ones? We have anxieties, but have we quite got to the bottom of what are the threats inherent in the way our young people have access to and use digital technology? We'll explore that in the next two chapters.

Something for you to try

Do these anxieties accord with your experience or do you have others? Try this quick exercise to see what relates to you, what does not and whether you feel you would like more information about the issue. If you want to know more about some possible approaches, and where to get more information, we will be dealing with much of this and signposting places to get more help later in the book.

	This worries me	This doesn't worry me	I need to know more
Access to pornography and violence			
Technical know-how			
Extra on the bills			
Downloading viruses			
When do they need protection			
Selfies and sexting			
Body image			
Cyberbullying			
Communication and family cohesion			
Distraction			
Life, but not as we know it			
It takes up too much time			
Drawing the line			
Parental consistency			
Dumbing down			
They pay more attention to friends			
Not knowing what they're up to			
You're losing control			
Your own digital use			

You will find at the end of the book an appendix listing organisations that will provide help on these topics as well as further reading.

3

The impact of the digital world on the family

"I was always a bit laid back about my son's involvement with the internet and social media until three boys in his class were found to have been collecting sexts of girls in the school. They apparently had hundreds. Some of the girls had found out and told parents who were up in arms. Two of the boys were given a police caution, and one a final warning because he'd put some on the internet. Which I was surprised to learn was not a soft option. It means that the incident was logged and was really going to spoil their chances in life – it would for instance make it impossible to work in professions such as law or teaching. I gave my son the telling off of all time saying he'd better not have been involved, he better not ever do anything like that and from now on there will be rules. He was very meek!"

Naomi, mother of 17-year-old boy

In Chapter 5 we will be exploring the positive aspects of digital technology. From the research we have done for this book we are clear that there are as many benefits and opportunities in the digital world as there are threats. We certainly don't want to give an entirely negative view. But in order to understand and get control of digital technology and how we and our children may be using it, the second step, having considered what anxieties we have found most parents express, is to look at what might be the real concerns about digital use. We've divided these into two sections in this and the next chapter. Firstly we'll look at what perhaps you should be worried about.

As we have seen, many parents have a range of anxieties about digital use. But are these fears justified? The reality is that many young people are digital natives, brought up with these devices, taking them for granted. Many of the older generation are digital immigrants – inexperience and lack of confidence could make them unnecessarily cautious. And a sizeable and growing group of parents are in the middle – we have grown up with digital technology as it developed, we use it a lot but perhaps don't have quite the total immersion that comes with having been born to smart phones and tablets. And the very fact we take it for granted almost as much as our children may indeed make the threats more covert and thus more dangerous. Because yes, we should be worried and in this chapter we shall look at the mounting evidence that suggests unfettered and unconsidered access to digital media can create problems for young people, their parents and society at large. As in so many things, it's not the thing itself that is bad, it's how we use or misuse it that brings up worrying issues.

Parents responding to our online survey told us that their children were 'fully wired'. Typical reports were that their children ". . . have phones and laptops. My son also has his own tablet and the school have just provided everyone in his year with a school tablet. We also have a games console."

> "We have to accept that our children live in a different world and, whether we like it or not (and I suspect most of us really don't), their social lives are intertwined with social media and their devices. You can't know everything they're up to and you shouldn't want to, a bit like not reading someone's diary in my day. So we need to let go to an extent."
>
> Phil, father with three children of 9, 14 and 16

Some parents do let go. Others join in – one newspaper columnist gleefully reported she loved using social media and mobile phones to be in touch with her children – it was so much easier texting her kids to tell them dinner is ready than standing at the foot of the stairs and shouting. Better still, of course, might have been making the kitchen the heart of the family and having them take part in making dinner, thereby gaining valuable skills, probably banishing faddy eating, while chatting and strengthening family bonds . . . Yet others try to hold back the waves, seeking to ban, block or otherwise control their young people's internet access.

So what are the real issues to consider that should raise anxieties?

The amount of screen time, and when it begins

"My seven month old is already fascinated by screens and displays even though we don't allow him to watch tv but as parents we spend almost every moment on iPad, phone, or computer for our work so he does get to see a screen a lot. He already knows that if you touch most screens something interesting happens. We haven't yet started working out what rules or how we'll work them – we will, at some point."

Joanna, new parent

"We were very aware of not putting the TV on too much in front of the little one but what we didn't realise is that there are screens everywhere (computer, iPads, phones etc.) so our children do get introduced to these devices when they are really young so they think it's normal and safe. We really need to educate them about the dangers."
Rosie mother of 12-month and 2-year-old daughters

What many of us don't recognise until it is too late is the ubiquity of screens and digital devices, and the ease of access to the internet and social media. Therein lies one of the threats. It is really very hard to shield young people from all of this. We may tell ourselves they are protected if we don't actually allow our young children to touch the objects themselves. But we use them so they see them, and see us using them, from birth. And of course, more and more it seems to be assumed that children will want to use them and will be allowed use them from a very early age. You can now buy pushchairs with slots for tablets. Babies are learning to operate devices from a few months old and there are thousands of apps targeting children under 3, based on nursery rhymes, games or learning the alphabet. These include:

- Soothing noises said to help your baby relax and sleep better. Sounds include a car ride, classical music and sounds from the womb.
- A cat that purrs or yowls when stroked, and repeats everything you say.
- Balloon animals that you inflate by blowing into the microphone on your phone and construct by shaking your phone.
- A virtual peekaboo game that makes animal sounds when you tap the graphic.
- A game to encourage children to tidy up – spin a wheel to find a tidy-up task, be rewarded by faster music and stars if you do the task quickly.

One of the significant measures of social change is how some things are portrayed in advertisements. Even in ads that aren't there to sell an app or a device, very young small children – even babies – are now regularly shown looking at or manipulating smart phones or tablets. Lucy told us of seeing a 2-year-old child touching the TV screen in his home and clearly not understanding why nothing happened. And Simon told us another 'funny story' of his 2-year-old nephew ". . . having a sulk the other day. Bottom lip trembling, arms out, 'I. . . . .Pad'. 'I. . . . .Pad' " Simon didn't find it at all funny. He knows that more and more psychologists and medical practitioners are sounding warnings about the age at which children should be allowed to have 'screen time'. According to some reports, exposure to screens before the age of 2 is associated with impaired learning, increased impulsivity and a decreased ability to self-regulate tantrums and other negative behaviours.

Parents may feel it almost impossible to limit screen time, given that we use so many devices in their presence. There is enormous social pressure to see digital use at a young age as normal with apps and programs, films and audio targeted at very young children – or, at their parents with the implication that you are doing yourself and your child a favour by using them. What parent hasn't heaved a sigh of relief at having a quiet moment from toddlers because the television is babysitting? How beguiling to have new methods in flashing lights and cooing sounds do the same on tablet and phone to a crying baby?

Using media to give us some time as well as giving in to their demands can mean that parents take their eye off the ball about just how often and how long their children are looking at screens. And, of course, what they may be viewing. We have an agreed 'watershed' in the UK where adult content is not screened on television before 9pm. However, with access to the internet viewers can watch 'on demand', which means actual broadcast times are now irrelevant. If your child has an internet-enabled screen in their bedroom or access to a DVD player to go with a television or computer, or a games console, they can watch or play whatever they like, whenever they like. Unless you monitor and supervise.

Some parents seem to feel that playing games is less of a worry than being on the internet.

"They were allowed to be online until 9pm weeknights, 10:30pm weekends. The boys were more into games consoles, which had the same curfew, but less strictly."
Brian, father of a 13-year-old daughter
and sons 12 and 16

Maybe he, like so many parents, hadn't realised that games consoles are portals to the internet too.

Parents we surveyed said time online for their children varied from:

- 24/7
- an 11-year-old with 15 hours a week and a 13-year-old with closer to 40
- until 9pm weekdays, 10.30pm weekends
- a 9-year-old with 30 minutes per day plus homework and 2–3 hrs television but 30 minutes reading

- a 17-year-old with 4 hours per day
- a 14-year-old with 5 hours per day, more at weekends
- 7 hours access but none after 9pm, Saturday all day, Sunday none

More screen time, less sleep time

"I really worry about sleep vs time on devices. They're on 24/7, literally, the phone is within reach, even on the bed while he's sleeping. At school, unless a teacher demands it, their phones are on. At work, I notice all the young people check their phones, all the time."

Bella, mother of 15-year-old son

According to research by Ofcom, the communications regulator in the UK:

- We spend twice as long online as we did a decade ago.
- The biggest increase over the last five years has been amongst 16- to 24-year-olds, tripling their usage.
- More than 25% of internet users watch TV or films online, compared to one in ten in 2007. Watching video clips online has almost doubled over eight years from 21% to 39% of internet users.
- The use of social media has tripled since 2007. Nearly 75% of internet users aged 16 and over say they have a social media profile compared with 20% in 2007.

But why should we be worried about young people using screens? Researchers suggest too much screen time is detrimental to children's psychological health and neurological development. One of the biggest studies on the effects of the digital revolution on children, by Public Health England (PHE), concluded that children who spent more than four hours a day in front of the television or a computer screen were more likely to develop anxiety or depression. "The greater the time spent in front of the screen, the greater the negative impact on behavioural and emotional issues relating to development," says Kevin Fenton, director of health and wellbeing at PHE.

There are several issues here. One is the effect of a flickering, lighted screen on brain development. Another is that lit screens are likely to inhibit sleep, a major concern for parents. The sedentary life style that can result from excessive screen use can lead to risk of diabetes, high blood pressure and shorter sleep duration because children do not feel tired out from exercise to get to sleep on time.

"We have lots of arguments about the amount of time they spend on their computers. We set limits but there are frequent disagreements on these, and some days it just seems my entire life is a screaming row. I hate it. We recently decided to be tough and say they could use it Saturday morning while I'm shopping but after that they can check messages once for an hour and Sunday is family day – no devices. Boy, did we have arguments about that, at first."

Gina, mother of 12-year-old daughter
and 17-year-old son

Parents can then find themselves in a vicious cycle. Given the choice between going to sleep or playing one more round of an exciting game, or watching an engrossing film or set of video clips, most children will opt for the latter, insisting they're 'not tired'. Most parents are aware that 4–5-year-olds need 10 to 12 hours sleep and 7–12-year-olds need 9 to 10½ hours a night. But do we all realise teenagers need 9¼ hours? They're often the ones who are sleep deprived because they insist on keeping adult hours, saying they can't sleep and staying up till midnight. Parents can be fooled either into taking their word for it or fail to monitor when lights or screens are turned out.

"As parents we try and limit time spent on devices. We have found that we have to police use or the device doesn't get switched off promptly."

Sonia, mother of 9- and 11-year-old daughters

A child who stays up late may get up on time for school but feel cranky and exhausted so perform so much less well than they should. And their bad mood and yours leads to conflict and arguments that make the situation worse. One solution is to set down, agree and enforce bedtimes, and a bedtime routine – more on that later. But another, when it comes to teenagers, might be to encourage your children's school to look again at their timetable. Research does indicate that teenagers have a biological predisposition to go to sleep at about midnight and get up late. They are not fully awake until between 9am and 10am, more than two hours later than adults. They learn more in the afternoon if allowed to follow such a routine. Several schools in the UK are at the time of writing experimenting with allowing teenage pupils to start later – some at 11.30am, or shifting school hours to 10am to 5.30pm. But . . . they still have to go to bed in time to get that 9¼ hours!

Parental engagement and family involvement

"We had awful problems last year and we put it down to our oldest son spending so much time online. It wasn't until I had a long and involved discussion with one of his teachers that I had to face up to the fact that his biggest problem was the arguments his father and I were having. He went online to escape. He spent so much time online and he was depressed. But chicken and egg – the depression was what made him go online, not the other way round. We got some help, we got on better, home became a much nicer place for all of us and hey presto! he wasn't online so much."

Mother with son of 16

As has been mentioned, research shows "The greater the time spent in front of the screen, the greater the negative impact on behavioural and emotional issues relating to development", according to the director of health and well-being at Public Health England. But it's just as likely that young people who spend so much time immersed online can be doing it for reasons that themselves contribute to behavioural and emotional issues. Sometimes, the way to get your child off the internet is not to ban it but to find out why else they may be gravitating towards it, and why else such problems may be arising. It's often tempting to blame an external influence than look at what might be happening in the family, between parents and between parent and child, that could need the fix.

Short attention span

> "I'm not sure if I'm idealising the past but sometimes it feels as if my two simply can't keep their minds on anything for more than a few minutes. Were we like that? We were trying to put up a bookcase in my youngest's bedroom the other day and he looked at the actually quite simple but fairly long instruction sheet and threw it away, saying he couldn't be bothered. I went through it and did the task but he couldn't or wouldn't put his mind to it."
>
> Josh, sons aged 12 and 15

Using digital technology, especially access to the internet and social media, has led to a rise in multitasking. As teenagers we probably argued with parents that we could do our homework or revision better with music blaring or the television on. Now, children expect to watch programmes on screens, tweet, blog, update social media and text while working – as do many adults. Indeed, multitasking has come to be seen as healthy and helpful – working, watching, doing the weekly shop at the same time seems super-efficient. While there is some truth in that, some psychologists think information overload can be detrimental. They note a curious phenomenon – some of the most successful people in the arts and business world far from being always on, are always off. They use notebooks and pens and landline phones. Unlike so many people they give their brains the chance to daydream and rest rather than overtaxing them. The argument is that apparently skilled multitaskers are simply better at switching between tasks – most people find too many calls on their attention lowers their ability to concentrate and be productive. And is it having a general effect? Game producers say they now know to keep instructions very short and sweet. The present generation of gamers, unlike the last, cannot be expected to read more than a line or two. You may have noticed the increase, indeed, in instructional videos rather than text in many contexts from recipes to DIY. Multitasking and constant switching between various tasks and feeds may mean we find it so much harder to concentrate on one thing for any length of time.

Not being able to be bored

"When I was young and complained 'I'm bored!' my mother would shout 'Bored is boring – go and find something to do!' And I would."

Suzie Hayman, with 48-year-old stepson and 9-year-old granddaughter

Do young people allow themselves the time to get bored anymore? Or do they reach for phone, tablet, game console, to play, chat, post, download and upload? This has had some interesting associated effects. According to the Office for National Statistics, half the number of girls under 18 become pregnant now than did 25 years ago. Over the same period consumption of illegal drugs has also halved, teenagers drink a third less alcohol and most teenagers do not smoke. But is this the good news it seems to be? Why did young people drink, smoke, have sex? Mostly, because they were bored and it was either something to do or part of something to do – hanging out with equally bored friends. Instead, they now reach for a screen.

Never getting bored can arguably be as destructive as drinking, smoking and having early sex. It can mean young people growing up with few personal resources – they never have to use their imaginations or work at making choices to find something to do. Contemplation and original thought, exploring different solutions and new ideas and above all building up face-to-face connections and learning how to negotiate and compromise, can go by the board.

Face-to-face friendships and communication

"I'm a Luddite by nature and most days I wish the internet and mobile phones had never happened. I try not to see their lives through the prism of someone who had a 70s/80s childhood but I wish they'd spend a bit more time doing physical activities and a bit less time locked into their screens."

Amal, mother of 8- and 11-year-old daughters
and 13-year-old son

As well as opting for screentime rather than sleep, children given the option will often choose devices over spending time with family, or indeed face-to-face with friends. Family Lives has heard disturbing reports from nursery and infant school staff about children who, when addressed, look down, as if seeking a screen rather than up to the speaker's face. In the same way, we hear from parents and other adults about coming upon groups of teenagers, in your own home or in public, who all seem to be concentrating on their devices rather than talking to the people they are with. Eye contact is something babies and children seek and respond to, but also something they need to learn, by experiencing it. Similarly, face-to-face communication needs to be experienced and learnt. The more children spend time with the people in their lives having this interaction the more they learn how to share, how to empathise, how to manage emotions and relationships. These are key factors in reducing childhood anxiety and conflict. Instead, social media teaches users to expect short bursts of information. It is said that 90% of communication is in body language, tone and facial expression. If you're only seeing 10% you are at a disadvantage. There is no nuance, no genuine intimacy and little connection. Instead, posting status updates via social media keys into an innate need for acceptance and to be 'liked'. What happens, however, when one status update gets 20 likes, but the next gets zero or minimal likes? We have certainly heard of children becoming depressed over this. It may be what drives many of them to go to some lengths to be noticed, by posting outrageous, exaggerated claims.

Too much screen time can also lead to a highly mechanistic outlook on life. Children may begin to think that events in life and other people can be controlled, as they can in a game, and that results should be instantaneous, as they often are online. Important emotional skills could be undermined as children lose the ability to socialise and begin to think that they could exercise control and receive instant gratification.

Conflict in the family

"Our children certainly resent having to switch off their phones and tablets, at mealtimes or at bedtime. We do have raging rows about it sometimes – I'll catch them at night when they should be asleep still talking to their friends on social media. I ask them to switch off when they come home and I find them texting under the table while I'm trying to chat about their day and I just lose it. And they scream back, and that's the evening gone."

Charlotte, mother of 13-year-old son
and 15-year-old daughter

Conflict between parent and child is as old as are families, and has a multiplicity of causes and reasons. But digital devices and social media – or rather, how we manage them – don't help. Devices that connect you to the outside world have several effects on family cohesion. Both parents and children can resent the way their family members are willing to spend time with other people than them, not only outside the home but when in it. They can feel rejected, resentful and ignored. Both can feel they have to respond to the demands of social media, replying to and paying attention to outside connections, while their face-to-face connections feel their needs are ignored. Bitterness can result in both parties resorting to anger and quarrels, as the only way they can get their requests for attention recognised and acted upon. Once either side finds the only way they can get attention is by shouting or arguing, you can become locked in a cycle of conflict as you all learn negative attention is the only attention you are likely to get.

Conflict can also be fuelled when either parents or adults appeal to other people's opinions – "Why can't you be more like so-and-so", "My friend says you're so unfair!", "Everyone at school can do it, why can't I?". It was bad enough when adults and children knew their arguments were shared and commented on by friends and other family members, after the event, via word of mouth. Now, both sides can upload comments or even audio or videos of an argument and appeal for support. So called "parent shaming" or "child shaming" may seem very funny at the time, and quite reassuring as people who are not just in your own social circle but around the world join in telling you what awful parents or ghastly children you have. It's not so funny or reassuring when both sides can continue smarting over the loss of trust and the lasting humiliation this can cause. One thing that needs to be recognised by anyone using the internet and social media is that there is no real delete button. "Charlie bit my finger" is an amusing video a father uploaded in 2008 showing a baby biting his older brother's finger. Seven years later it had had over eight million views and was the most viewed video bar some music videos. The brothers, revisited seven years later, were relaxed about the fact that they had worldwide notoriety. They may feel differently as teenagers. Other parents and children have found it really hard to forgive such public shaming.

FOMO – fear of missing out

"My children do actually understand and they do accept in principle what we're saying. The problem is there is so much pressure on them to keep up with their friends. My daughter said to me a few weeks ago she would quite like not having to be on her phone for a while. But only – and here's the whole point – if everyone else did it."

Tim, father of an 11-year-old son and
15-year-old daughter

Possibly the biggest pressure on anyone using social media is Fear Of Missing Out. If you're not there, you fear, your friends will be talking behind your back and you will become the butt of the jokes. Or that the people there will bond more strongly, leaving you an outsider. Anyone involved in online gaming will know the anxiety of what happens if you're out of the game for any period – your character may be killed off, defeated or taken over by someone else. It's the biggest driver to keep online and thus possibly the biggest threat. It's what keeps people reaching for their phones an estimated 50 to 200 times a day and leads to them taking them into the bedroom to be left on all the time. Even kids who have been cyberbullied are most reluctant to come offline. As one said, "They think I'm different and odd enough already. If I wasn't there I'd be a total loser."

"We don't allow them to have devices in their room at night. My son is quite active in trying to circumvent that rule although he rarely questions the case for it. I know a lot of his friends don't have the same restrictions and are up very late on social media etc. We also have a rule about switching devices off half an hour before bedtime but we haven't been so good at enforcing it (partly because we have our own phones on at the same time)."

> Hannah, mother of 15-year-old daughter
> and 17-year-old son

Gaming

"To be honest, I've been playing games for years and it's now something my two sons and I can share, settling down on a rainy weekend afternoon to do together."

> Gordon, father of sons aged 11 and 13

Gaming is a multibillion pound industry. Many young people will play some sort of game at some time in their childhood and often into adulthood. Their involvement can range from a once-a-week dabble with a game on a DVD at home to complete immersion in a massively multiplayer online role-playing game (MMORPG) where players, often from around the world, meet in an online virtual world to interact with one another.

Gaming rewards focus and attention in a fast-paced environment with regular gratification. Game designers use psychologists to help them design games that keep people playing and striving to advance. They do this by offering frequent rewards and satisfaction, personal as well as story development and the knowledge that the more you try the better you can be and the more you can win. One of the drawbacks is that traditional school work can seem tame and unresponsive in comparison and kids can lose interest in that aspect of their lives if gaming is something they do often. Young people can get hooked on obsessive behaviour so they neglect studies and indeed neglect everything except the game and the people they meet there.

The reality is that young people love to be competitive. When faced with an anti-competitive ethos, as in many schools that perhaps laudably seek to reward everyone for trying rather than the few for coming top, it may be no surprise to find many young people opting to seek gaming opportunities either in DVDs or apps, or on the net.

Gaming itself may be less of a threat than you might think – we'll explore the advantages of it in the next chapter. The danger arises in two aspects – when gaming is unrestrained and young people can become so involved everything else in their lives takes a back seat. And when the games they play are inappropriate.

Just as with films, games come with an age rating. Age ratings are systems used to ensure that entertainment content, such as films, videos, DVDs, and computer games, are clearly labelled for the age group for which they are most suitable. Games are rated by PEGI – Pan European Game Information ratings. They are:

- 3 (suitable for all age groups)
- 7 (for 7s and over)
- 12 (for 12s and over)
- 16 (16s and over)
- 18 (adults only)

Additional information tells you if scenes:

- contain violence
- contain bad language
- might inspire fear
- might refer to drug use
- are sexual
- could encourage discrimination
- encourage or teach gambling
- can be played online with other people

Some shops will ask for proof of age and refuse to sell games and videos to children below the rated age, and some will ask adults buying if it is for a child and if so what age. But most will leave it to the adult concerned, which is why it really is essential for parents to understand the ratings and act on them. Games designed for over 18s almost certainly come with backstories that contain attitudes to violence and drug taking and sexual content that are not suitable for 11-year-olds.

Drinking

"My wife has a photo of me, taken 30 years ago by my bloody mother, when I was 18 years old on holiday and 'nished as a pewt'! She has it hidden away and says it's her insurance; if I step out of line she'll show it to our two daughters. I'm so glad we didn't have social media in my day!!!"

Jacques, daughters aged 7 and 11

What do young people upload to the internet and look for on social media? Cat images seem to dominate. And porn. And music. And, pictures of drunken revelry.

Research from the charity Drinkaware has revealed:

- 39% children aged 10–17 who use social networking sites report seeing images of their friends drunk.
- 13% children as young as 10–12 years old who use social networking sites report seeing images of their friends drunk.

Young people have always gone for the "We're mad, us" approach and delight in showing themselves and their friends having as crazy and out of control a time as possible. Now they have cameras on their phones and to hand, and can access the internet and upload their pictures at once with a few taps. So the area of social media annexed by under 25-year-olds is awash with drunk pix. Does it matter? Yes, massively, on several counts. The study for Drinkaware conducted by Ipsos MORI showed online networking sites could have a significant influence on young people's perceptions of normal drinking behaviour – everyone does it so we should too. The influence of their peer group increases steeply with age:

- 7% of 10–11-year-olds report being encouraged to drink by someone their age or younger.
- 19% of 10–17-year-olds say that all or most of their friends drink alcohol.
- 37% 15–17 years old report being encouraged to drink by someone their age or younger.

Another threat is that those pictures remain. Some colleges and some employers now use the internet to research potential students or employees. Pictorial proof of behaviour that could suggest you may not be reliable can blight your prospects.

Airbrushing reality

"My sister has always been someone who doesn't let reality get in the way of a good story. But lately I've been quite worried about her. It's not just that she tells awful fibs on her Facebook page about what she's been doing, it's that I think she can't quite tell the difference between what she says happened and what really happened. Is she losing it?"

Letter to Suzie Hayman on *Woman* magazine's agony page

Social media brings with it a constant demand for updating. You're invited to tweet, to post status updates, to join in and say what you're doing and what you think. It's like being round a cafe table, chatting away. Not posting means you're not there. And if you're not there joining in the chat you risk being the one gossiped about. Or, as people now seem to fear, simply fading away and ceasing to exist.

The danger is that the pressure is on to always come up with something entertaining or interesting or at least new. You get constant and often immediate feedback – what you say can attract 'likes' or 'favourites' or replies or 'shares'. It can make someone's day when they attract 20 'likes' to an update – depress them when something goes unremarked upon. The temptation is to post exaggerated stories to attract 'likes' or attention, airbrushing reality to please your audience. But research suggest this has an unfortunate side-effect. We may all be familiar with the confusion about recalling popular family stories. Do I remember the time I was in my baby buggy and let go of a red balloon and we followed it over a zebra crossing? Or is it that I've heard my mother tell the story so many times the image conjured has acquired the status of memory? Tell a story and invest in it, and you may come to believe your lies. By lying on social media sites such as Facebook and Twitter, users may 'rewrite' their memories. We've heard from people who feel sadness and shame as a result of not being able to live up to their online image, but also are genuinely confused about what was and was not real.

Shopping and acquiring

"They aren't able to buy anything online (although this doesn't stop them downloading illegally or semi-legally). My brother had the shock of his life a couple of years ago when his son spent £1000 on in-app purchases in a game on a new tablet. In the event, the provider was very good about refunding it but it certainly taught us all a lesson!"

Bella, mother of 15-year-old son

When parents think of their children spending time online, their first concern is to protect them from unwanted content on the web. However, there is another important aspect that should not be forgotten. That is when they look for things they most definitely want, and it costs you much more than you thought. Games played online, on laptops, tablets, consoles or mobile phones, can offer upgrades and other purchases as the child plays. If you've allowed the device to be set up to bill you without a further password, a child who simply doesn't understand the implications can say yes, until the bill arrives or you get texted alarms. But young people may also allow their desire for an item to overcome their sense and caution, if they have access to your credit card or password. They may indeed hope you don't check all purchases closely, or just ignore the fact that there will be a reckoning – one day soon! Mobile phone apps may appear not on a credit card bill but your phone bill – you do have to check everything. And of course, children can cost you a lot of money if they either delete important information or download viruses while using the family computer or their own. You don't only need to have up-to-date and efficient virus control but to heed any warning the program gives you.

You may feel your child would never do something like this. Beware of the power of peer pressure. Young people share all sorts of ideas, hints and tips. Some of these may relate to the ease and methods of buying online. This could result in their feeling it's common and natural and justifiable to step over this particular line. The problem is that it only takes one crazy moment to run up an astounding bill, and you may not be able to have it rescinded.

It may not have to be them with their finger on the buy button, however. Pester power is a potent force and 2015 research published by Mother's Union carried out by ComRes with over 1,000 parents in Great Britain shows that 81% of parents say their children ask them to buy them things that they see advertised. The 'vloggers' – people who post regular videos online – they may follow can be making their money by 'recommending' brands and items, or pushing their own products. And social media is now full of sponsored advertising that will show them items they want. They can be relentless in demands, and the ease with which you can order online may result in you doing the purchasing for them, if you don't think it through carefully.

Catching behaviour

"I can't keep up with all the crazy stuff my kids are either doing or at least tweeting about all the time. Drinking games, dares, challenges – it's just mad."

Mo, father of 16- and 18-year-old sons

The evolutionary biologist Richard Dawkins coined the word 'meme' to explain the spread of ideas and cultural phenomenon. He meant fashion, catchphrases, melodies and technology – how to build an arch, for instance, which arrived in many cultures at similar times. Memes are ideas, behaviour, styles that spread from person to person in a culture, or across many cultures, in the same way a virus can be catching and spread. The internet is full of examples of memes. The concept explains why young people may suddenly be joining what could be a community-wide, country-wide or even worldwide movement to do something. We call it 'going viral' when something on the internet achieves this sort of popularity and universal sharing.

Some memes are inspiring – more about those later – but some can be foolish and dangerous – punch4punch, neknominate, balconing, cinnamon challenge all showed people doing what could be harmful or dangerous challenges from which people have died (punch4punch, in which people trade a blow; neknominate, in which someone 'necks' an alcoholic or soft drink, and challenges a friend to go one better; balconing, where people jump from the balcony of a hotel room or flat to another, or into a swimming pool below; the cinnamon challenge where you must eat a spoonful of cinnamon in under 60 seconds – far more dangerous than it sounds). Others can be simply silly or dangerous if done in the wrong place. For instance planking, which involved lying straight, like a plank – benign if done on park seat, not so much if done on railway line or across two balconies.

Getting fat

"I do remember when we were young we really would take a sandwich and our bikes and go out all day. Sometimes we'd go into a phone box and call home to say we were ok – if it rained, for instance. Like as not, mum would just say 'Oh aye!' I can't imagine my grandchildren being allowed to do that now, even if they wanted to."

Graham, father of two adult sons and four grandchildren

Many parents fear their children would be unsafe if allowed out on their own. While our children's great grandparents probably thought nothing of walking or cycling six or more miles to explore or play, their grandparents probably found it similarly normal to go several miles but their parents only quarter of a mile to a local park. Children today are often confined to their own gardens or maybe to the end of their street, or indoors.

According to the Walk to School Campaign, in 1971, 80% of 7- and 8-year-olds made their own way to school without an adult; by 2006 this had dropped to 12% of 7- to 10-year-olds. Even at the age of 11, only about half of children walk to school unaccompanied. And there have been cases reported of schools taking parents to task for letting their children walk on their own, implying it is neglectful and dangerous. While some parents cite increased traffic as their reason for caution the main reason given is the risk of abduction and murder by paedophiles. But is this rational? The famous cases are terrifying, but they are also incredibly rare.

According to an analysis of official figures by the NSPCC:

- 53 children on average are killed at the hands of another person every year and of those the killer in more than two-thirds of cases is a parent or step-parent.
- In 2010–11, 77% of victims aged under 16 knew the prime suspect and 64% were killed by a parent or step-parent.
- In only 12% of cases was the killer a stranger.
- Teenagers or 'tweens', the age groups most constrained, are not the ones most at risk. The highest risk is to children under five (68% of all the deaths), with those under the age of one being more at risk than any other age group.

Kidnap and sexual abuse by a stranger is also rare and does not seem to have increased – statistics are difficult to unravel because abductions where a parent or other relative took a child away, even for a few hours, are included.

The problem is that we are swapping the very rare possibility of risk to children of being outdoors away from their parent's supervision for the very real likelihood of health risks, both mental and physical, of a sedentary lifestyle. Obesity has increased, conditions that result from unhealthy lifestyles such as diabetes have increased. While road traffic incidents have decreased, accidents in the home have gone up. The final outcomes would seem to suggest that our children are far more at risk staying at home than they might be if we let them roam free.

Identity and disclosure

As we've already said, Everything Is Shared on the internet. That might include your home address, and the jolly email that tells your friends – oh, and an awful lot of other people – that you'll be away on holiday for two weeks. Or the social media post put up by your child that alerts their closest acquaintances that you are away for the weekend, let's party (and 200 or maybe even a thousand young people turn up to wreck the joint . . .). What about those quizzes on social media that offer to tell you your favourite colour or what *Game of Thrones* character you are? In answering you give away a stunning amount of detail about yourself that can identify you, your passwords and online presence. We tell young people to be wary and not let slip details that could show where they live or what school they go to – and then allow them to post photos that could do exactly that. Or, more important, we 'Sharent'. Sharenting is the modern equivalent of getting out the photo album when friends come round, or sending pictures to nearest and dearest. Except, we do it online. From their birth, parents may get into the habit of taking and posting all sorts of pictures of their children – in school uniform, in fancy dress costume . . . in the buff. Cute for the grandparents; joyous for paedophiles and other people up to no good. If you are going to sharent, it's worth being careful about the privacy settings you establish. Do you want only friends, or friends and their friends, or the whole world to have access? And thinking carefully about whether your children will thank you in ten years' time for sharing that particular photo as widely as you did. When you disclose anything, in any way, ask yourself and your children to consider:

- Where does this go?
- Who may see it?
- Who might use it?

- Do I really want to share this with the world?
- Have I asked the people involved whether they consent too?

Our own use of the internet

"The first thing my partner and I do when we arrive home in the evening – and over weekends when we've been out, too – is to check emails, texts, social media, you name it. And we tend to check in every so often throughout the evening. I have awful battles with my kids over their bringing devices to the table, but I suppose I only have myself to blame."

Sara, mother of 17- and 11-year-old sons and
a 14-year-old daughter

There is one overriding rule for dealing with young people; "Do as I say not as I do" doesn't work. If you want to pass on healthy messages and wise lessons, you first have to look at your own behaviour and consider what sort of a model you are offering. Many of the parents who contacted us or with whom we discussed this issue either realised or let slip that their own use of digital technology was less than ideal:

"I dropped and broke our alarm clock last year and haven't bothered replacing it because I use my mobile phone. Problem is that has meant my wife has taken to bringing hers to bed also and we both check them far too often. When I tried to bar my son from taking his new smartphone into his bedroom he had me – he said why was it one rule for him and another for us? Telling him it's different for adults cut no ice, and the truth is he was right."

Nigel, father of 12-year-old boy

They do as you do, not as you say. If you show them you cannot be without a device and spend as much if not more attention on people outside the family than within, they will follow your example and it's no use complaining. If you feel excluded, rejected, ignored, alienated, sidelined by your children's use of digital tech the first strategy you need to explore is whether they are only aping what they have experienced with you. If so, amend your own behaviour before you ask them to think about theirs.

Anxieties, actual and perceived

As you can see from this and the previous chapter, there are some differences in our worries about our children's digital use, and the actuality. We need to ask ourselves whether our concern is because what they might encounter and what they might do is real, pervasive and dangerous or whether there are other reasons for our fears. One of the main attractions for young people is that using digital technology gives them a measure of control. They can do something we struggle with – that has appeal. But also they can search out information or be in touch with friends without having to ask your permission and this can cause us concern. However, on top of these worries, there may be greater risks out there – real threats. We'll consider them in the next chapter.

Something for you to try

Talk through the issues in this chapter with your partner, with friends, with adult family members – do you share the same level of concern about the same issues or do you have different attitudes? If so, discuss why some of you may feel more worried than others.

4

The actual threats of the digital world

In Chapter 2 we looked at what anxieties parents generally express about their children and digital use. In Chapter 3 we explored the reality – what issues perhaps you should be worried about. Now we'll turn to the more serious aspects of digital use and the internet, and look at what might be the dark side of what could otherwise be fun and games.

Internet addiction

"My son started with a games console we gave him, after nagging, for Christmas. Two years later he had a smart phone, a laptop and tablet as well. And we never saw him. When his grandparents came from Canada last Easter he spent the whole time tapping on his phone. So one day when he was at school I cleared his room and locked everything up. I told him he was off everything for a month, except his tablet for homework and that would be under our eyes, and when he was allowed back it would be with rules and limits and nothing was allowed in his bedroom. He literally screamed at me for four hours, then refused to speak to us for ten days. And gradually the old child came back. He joined in. He laughed. And when the month was up he said he didn't want the console back again."

Serena, mother of 13-year-old son

In some people, the drive to keep up and continue online, whether on social media or gaming, can descend into addiction. Addiction is a state where someone continues to engage with a stimulus in spite of adverse consequences. That can be physical or mental ill health, relationship problems, financial or work- or education-related problems and more.

We tend to assume this refers to a chemical stimulus such as heroin or cocaine. In fact, behaviour can be addictive too. The key is that whatever it is, it is rewarding – at least, at first. Intermittent reward – frequent and satisfying – is the most powerful conditioning tool of all. And you can find that in plentiful supply on the internet. It comes when a post of yours on social media gets a reaction, positive or negative – it doesn't matter, it's a validating response. You get it when a post is 'favourited' or 'liked' or 'shared'. You get it in games – not just at the end but repetitively throughout, because game makers know that intermittent reward is what gets people continuing and coming back.

We have heard instances of people withdrawing from education, friendships and family interaction, of being sent down from university, of losing jobs because they become so immersed in their online life they have no time for real-world life. As with drugs, these forms of addiction are initially rewarding and satisfying. They then become less so as the person using them becomes both dependent and tolerant to the stimulus. You need more to give you the same high, and eventually the drug or the behaviour is needed to simply help you feel 'normal'. As with drug addiction, the reasons driving the person to seek solace in the behaviour can be complex and not readily understood and professional help may be needed to challenge and change the behaviour.

It's become an addiction when:

- you withdraw from other aspects of your life such as friendships, family, education or work
- use is causing problems – expense, loss of friendships, family conflict, failure in education or work
- the behaviour ceases to be a pleasure and becomes a necessity – you have to keep doing it to feel ok
- you need more of the behaviour to feel the same as you did with lower levels of it
- if you try to reduce the behaviour you experience discomfort

Cyberbullying

"My child was a victim of cyberbullying at school. It was swiftly dealt with by the head of year."

Mother of son now 21

"My daughter's head absolutely insisted his school did not have a bullying problem, no matter how many times we contacted him. When we produced evidence and he couldn't deny it was happening, he then switched tactics and said since it was online it was out of school (some of the nasty texts were clearly timed as having been sent during a school day!) so none of their responsibility. We took her out of school and eventually found somewhere better with a head who took her school's responsibility seriously. But although we rescued our child and she's fine now, I felt I'd failed as I left other children to bear the brunt of what was still going on."

Mother of a 13-year-old

Most parents have heard of cyberbullying – bullying through the medium of the internet and social media. It is a huge worry to many. However, parents might not realise just how bad it can be, and how powerful. It might be easy to spot physical bullying, with bruises and grazes, torn clothing or 'lost' belongings giving the game away. Even then, children will often deny there is a problem, blaming it all on accidents. Children who are bullied tend to accept the tormentor's assertion that they bring it on themselves – that they deserve to be pushed around for whatever reason the bully will pick out and target. Bullied children thus often feel shame and responsibility and hide what is happening even from their nearest and dearest and those who could help. Cyberbullying is several stages worse than this. It is psychological so doesn't leave obvious bruises. It can take place at any time, in any locale. While a child being beaten can come home and close the front door or bedroom door and feel safe, cyberbullying follows you home and pops up in your refuge – there is no refuge.

Bullying is nothing new – it has always existed and many positive advances have been made in tackling it, in schools and in the workplace. There are plenty of examples of good practice and all schools now have to have a bullying policy. However, having a policy does not seem to mean all schools put it into practice, either at all or effectively. And even though cyberbullying is actually easier to prove than physical bullying, many schools either don't understand the import of it or feel it is off school grounds so not their responsibility.

Cyberbullying can be posting jokes or insults about someone on their own social media page or on a social media site open to all, or in texts or messages. It can be threats of harm or even death, or instigations to harm themselves. It can be posting a fake invitation from the victim so that they get mails or posts taking up the offer placed in their name – often of an extreme sexual nature. It can be creating a whole website or social media page to invite as many people as possible to say they hate the victim or wish they were dead. It can, since so many young people have digital skills, be of (otherwise) admirable sophistication.

Online bullying is several stages more dangerous and harmful than real-world bullying, for quite a few reasons. One is the ubiquity of the platform. Hardly any young people are offline and, once on, however unpleasant the experience, very few are willing to come off. You might say "Just ignore it – don't go and look at what they are saying" but very few youngsters would be willing to do that.

Online access seems to be encouraging cyberbullying. Partly this is because being at arm's length of anything they say and not having to see the other person's face when they hear it, it's easy to escalate insults and remarks. Young people may not yet have fully developed the ability to be empathetic – they simply don't think what it might feel like to have these things said to them. Even if they do, the medium and the audience encourage them to reassure themselves it's just a joke and means nothing. A large part of the problem is the sheer scale, and the fact that it's often a complete stranger you are joining in hounding – not only can you not see their face, you won't have to do so next morning at your school. The sort of mob mentality that drives face-to-face bullying is multiplied in cyberbullying because so many people can become involved – people who know the victim being joined by people who do not, often not only in other towns or regions of the same country but other parts of the world.

Ringleaders of bullying very rarely work on their own. They need acolytes – helpers. These are usually the ones who actually administer the blows and the insults. Or, by being an audience, they cheer on and encourage the main protagonist. When you factor in the massive audience – it could actually be millions in some cases – who are part of this, it's easy to see how cyberbullying can get out of hand and extreme. Each one vies with others to go one better in the smart, wounding quip – it's a game. It's not real. Except to the victim. Being 'smart' and 'clever' in insults has become, to many of our young people, a way of life. After all, they see it all the time in reality television programmes and game shows. Dismissing someone with a witticism is the name of the game – and if adults do it on screen, young people feel they have permission to do so too. But when you add together this mob mentality with the anonymity of the internet and the ability to gather large numbers of people together this can tend towards bullying and aggression on a truly frightening scale.

Cyberbullying can also so much more easily become the resort of someone who has been bullied. People who bully never do so for the fun of it. They do it because at some point in their lives they have been exploited and abused – they have had the experience of feeling powerless and out of control. They bully someone else to get back a feeling of being confident and competent, and in command, which is sadly why people who have had it done to them can become the ones dishing it out. They may do so face-to-face, when they are older and bigger than when they experienced it. They may do so to peers or younger children, in reaction to being bullied at home or by older, bigger people. They may do it to younger members of their family, in response to being bullied at school. Or, they may find they can do so online when no-one can see them.

In a strange twist, some people have used the very anonymity of the internet to use cyberbullying to garner support, by posting anonymous insults directed at themselves, hoping that other users will jump in with reassurance and kindness.

Cyberbullying is a serious threat because so many applications on the internet seem to facilitate it. You'd almost come to believe, rather than simply not thinking it through, some designers have designed websites and mobile phone applications to make it easy to use them to make other people's lives difficult. There are websites that allow users to post anonymously. The positive reason is that it allows young people who have genuine anxieties – about sex and gender, about a myriad of issues that worry young people – to post a question and get an answer without disclosing their identity. Except, they have been used to post insults and innuendo about targeted individuals. One, the Yik Yak app, sparked a scandal in the US as high-school students used it to spread nasty messages about their fellow pupils. Users of the free app do not need to create a profile or provide a username, they can simply post an anonymous message visible to any other user within a 1.5-mile radius. The designers say that it was designed as a 'local bulletin board' to share funny and interesting news within a community, and will disable it within certain locations if asked. A significant number of US schools have had to ask just that, as very little funny or interesting news was shared, but an awful lot of insults and unpleasantness.

Ask your children to keep to these rules

We'll look at many more ways to help your children manage the online world in the final chapter. But for now, start with this.

When you're about to say something on a social media site, ask yourself:

- Would I say this to this person or any other person to their face?
- If someone said it to me, would I feel hurt or rejected or that they were ganging up on me?
- Would I be happy for my granny to see what I posted?

If the answer to these is 'NO!', 'YES!' and 'NO!', then DON'T PRESS 'SEND'.

Sexting

"Everyone at my school does it."

14-year-old girl

Sexting is the sending of sexually explicit texts and pictures. In their 2014 annual survey on teens and smartphones, *The Wireless Report*, the anti-bullying charity Ditch the Label reported that:

- 37% of 13- to 25-year-olds in the UK have sent a naked photo of themselves via a smartphone app.
- 15% of 13- and 14-year-olds have sent a naked selfie at least once.

While the primary pressure is on girls – we have heard from girls who say boys in their school expect you to supply a sext before they will consider asking for a date – boys are also under increasing stress to appear buff, and to be able to prove it with a gym-body snap. Or to appear virile, and prove it with an explicit snap of their genitals. Young people themselves can be quite blasé about sexting:

"Sexting is like writing someone a really sexually explicit love letter. It's immoral if you share people's naked pictures and ruin it for them, but otherwise it's not bad. It's not doing anyone any harm. It's your sexuality: you should be able to choose what you want to do with it."

16-year-old girl

However, the ubiquity of such photos and the ease with which they can be taken and sent makes it difficult for young people to stand back and dissent. As one said, "the girls who say it's cool are talking rubbish. They are self-protecting. They don't want to feel any feelings."

The problem is not the sexts themselves or the decision perhaps to share such intimacy with one person but what happens afterwards.

According to *The Wireless Report*:

- Nearly a quarter of 13- to 25-year-olds have had a naked photo shared without their consent.
- 5% of 13-year-olds send naked photos several times weekly.
- Nearly half believe that sexting is harmless fun.
- 13% said they felt pressured into doing it.

The apps that promise to automatically delete your snap, so you can share something explicit with someone secure in the idea that it can't be saved for them to show it to others or let it be distributed, have been found to be easily circumvented, either with clever work-arounds tech-savvy youngsters can operate or even by other apps. And supposedly secure storage can be cracked as well. In 2014 there was the so-called Fappening (fapping is internet slang for male masturbation) when female celebrities had videos and photos hacked from iCloud and posted online. This was followed by the Snappening when thousands of Snapchat photos and videos – the ones promised to have been deleted after a very short time – were leaked online including many explicit sexts sent by teens thinking they would vanish in ten seconds.

And of course, even if your young people are not involved in any of this, they are still growing up in a culture where this is what does happen, and may happen or has happened to people they know. Side by side with the almost overwhelming impulse to share and join in is the anxiety of what happens if and when it goes wrong.

Online sexual behaviour

"Porn is too easy so the game is to get girls to strip or do stuff on camera."

Teenage boy speaking to director Beeban Kidron in her groundbreaking documentary *InRealLife*

Following on from taking pictures or short videos of unclothed or sexual poses with mobile phones and posting them, either to contacts or on social media, young people can also get involved in carrying out sexual behaviour in front of web cameras.

These are used on porn sites – subjects will offer to strip and act sexually for viewers, for a consideration (credit card needed) of course. Young people who have seen or heard of this may then act out similar scenarios with friends or people they meet on the internet, either as viewer or viewee, or both. What the girl involved might initially think is her and her boyfriend, or prospective boyfriend, playing around with some affection and intimacy, can be far more abusive.

Acting from behind a screen can seem very safe – one wrong word or action, or simply feeling bored with that particular incident or that particular person, and you can click off. Pregnancy and sexually transmitted infections are impossible when it's screen sex. And if everyone is doing it, you might feel it has no blackmail potential and little shame attached. But no apparent risk can lead to risk-taking on several levels. A connection you felt was private can be made public – it can even go viral, where thousands or millions see it. That potential can be used as blackmail. But if it remains between the two of you, if and when you do meet, you've done the foreplay. That can mean you go straight on to satisfying sex with both partners confident and competent in knowing what they and the other likes and needs. Or, it can mean they feel they have to ramp up the action by going to extreme sexual acts.

Pornography

Most parents have heard about pornography being available and accessible on the internet, and do worry their children may be viewing inappropriate material. But do we worry enough? One difficulty seems to be that although there are anxieties, many parents often have no idea exactly how explicit such material may be and what is often part of the content. Some do – they use it themselves. But even then a certain amount of denial may take place when thinking about your own children accessing something similar.

Harry was reassuring when his wife said their 14-year-old son had been viewing pornography on his laptop – she discovered it because he'd been in a hurry to leave for school one day and failed to delete the history. "We watched blue movies and read top-shelf magazines," he said. "Never did us any harm!" But he was more than shocked when she showed him what their son had actually been viewing – sex involving a high degree of violence and hostility towards women and the abuse of young children. The reality is that pornography on the net is very different to that available in magazines or in films, even pornographic films, 10–20 years ago and must be treated as such. When you consider that the clothing, poses and actions performed in many music videos today would only be found in hardcore blue movies in the last generation, you might have some idea of what is available if you seek it out. Or, as some people find, ask questions of your search engines that prompt them to offer such sites. Of course, many parents don't view the videos that go with their children's favourite music. It's worth doing so.

You would think that pornography would be about sexual activity, showing men and women, or women and women, men and men, having sexual intercourse. You might have accepted that such images would only pay lip service to sexual relationships and mutual pleasure but at least assume that such existed. In fact, much of the pornography on the internet has suffered from the adage that any use of a stimuli, whether drug or behaviour, leads to tolerance – the diminishing effect resulting from repeated exposure. Tolerance leads to increased effect to get the same result. So, much internet pornography is of an extreme nature using not just sex but violence or quick images to get the desired response. On the whole, it shows men getting their pleasure with women as peripheral – not as people and not as part of mutual sensation but simply as providers.

Inappropriate content can be found in several ways. Friends, older siblings and school pupils can suggest sites or show content. When children do not have their questions about sex and sexuality answered at home or in school they can and now do go looking on the internet. They are then at risk of finding worrying, confusing and inaccurate answers in extreme pornography, which is then passed around the playground on a tablet or smartphone. Young people can ask innocent questions – such as a 13-year-old, naturally curious but stymied by a school that did not deal with the issue and parents too embarrassed, typing 'teenage sex' into a search engine . . . and getting far more and very different content to what he expected or wanted. And young people watching content on YouTube will find a menu of 'suggested videos' on the right, which have some connection to the one being viewed. The problem is when you follow one of those links, then another suggested link and then another – three clicks could lead you to all sorts of content, some of which could be explicit and unexpected.

One mother told us:

> "Our 9-year-old daughter watches music videos, some of which I have watched with her and am not happy about the content. We do have parental controls but we haven't put a password on preferring to talk to our child and operate on trust. We insist on computers and tablets being used in a public space in the home not behind closed doors. At the moment this is working fine."

But why is viewing porn a problem? Young people should be able to have their questions and curiosity about sexual matters answered and if parents and schools don't help them, the internet should be a good place to find out. The problem is that what they may find, whatever they ask, may well lead to something they didn't expect and actually didn't want. There are risks of young people seeing something that confuses and upsets them. If you've made them feel able to ask your input they may raise the issue, such as one respondent to Family Lives who told of her primary school child asking her "Why do you have to wear masks when you have sex?" More problematical is when children feel guilty about finding this sort of material and worry that you might be angry and tell them off, so they suffer their anxiety in silence.

Most worrying of all is the suggestion that many young people, since this may be the only or at least the major depiction of sex and sexual behaviour they see, are beginning to accept the attitudes and behaviour shown in pornography as normal. This is highly damaging to both boys and girls, men and women. Put sex and aggression together and you've soon got problems if it's being watched by teenagers at a very impressionable age. Young men can begin to think that sex is all about coming in a girl's face, not about intercourse or mutuality or loving, caring relationships. And once accepted, such attitudes are hard to alter. In her groundbreaking documentary *InRealLife* director Beeban Kidron showed two young teenagers watching a 20-second clip of a woman giving a man oral sex, saying afterwards "It was good to watch – her tits are perfect, that's what you'd look for. You'd try out a girl and want her to be exactly like the one you've watched and if she's not you move on."

The children's helpline ChildLine has said one in five 12–13-year-olds say watching online porn is 'normal behaviour' while almost one in 10 say they sometimes worry they are becoming addicted to it. In 2013–14 the pornographic website Pornhub was named one of the top five favourite sites by boys aged between 11 and 16. At the same time, young people post about 18,000 messages a month regarding exposure to porn on ChildLine discussion forums, suggesting they are anxious about the sorts of images they are viewing.

A 2011 Family Lives survey of over 1,000 parents of 8–17-year-olds found that 7% of respondents reported having experienced an issue with online pornography with their child, with 14% reporting that they had heard about this issue occurring with their child's friends or at their child's school. Most parents thought that they were the best person to talk to their children about pornography, although men were less likely to think so (64%) than women (76%).

Despite this, only 34% of parents had spoken to their child or planned to. In addition, where parents were prepared to speak to their children, many were leaving it until their children were older, with the average age that the conversation took place, or was expected to take place, being 13 years of age. Only 40% of parents felt that support and advice was available to help them talk to their child/ren about online pornography. 19% found little or no support or advice on the issue.

One of the major issues about pornography is that the concept of the watershed – the 9pm deadline before which content must be 'family friendly' – has no meaning with on-demand viewing, and with the number of young people able to view online ether through computers, mobile phones or other devices, in the privacy of their own rooms. Or indeed, handed round in the playground. This also means that the age at which young people first view such images, and there-fore begin to see them as normal, is falling.

It is now not uncommon for young girls to think sex involves being gagged, abused and slapped because these are the kind of clips that boys pass around the playground on their phones – hence, "Why do you have to wear masks when you have sex?" It's a macho, brutal vision of sex, acted out by impossibly toned and photogenic models of both sexes, which gives boys and girls issues not only about what they think sex should be like but what they should look like. The obsession with genital waxing – from leaving a narrow strip of hair to a full Brazilian or total depilation – which is now mainstream, started when pornography became so easily accessible.

During a seminar in which Hayman chaired a discussion session with Beeban Kidron, the director described a focus group she held with teenagers. At one point she asked them "Where would you 'come'?". She timed it and it took 20 min-utes, and some coaching and direct questions, before anyone said "In a woman's vagina". The 20 minutes had been spent saying "on her back", "on her chest", "in her face", "between her legs", "in her backside" – all sexual practices they had seen in pornography, and had internalised as "the way you do it". Learning about sex from porn is a bit like learning to drive by watching *The Fast and the Furious* series of films – all sliding, screaming and crashing. Real life is not like a CGI action movie, but for many young people sex is becoming normalised as something that is nasty, brutish and short and very much about men being serviced by women, to achieve quick and ultimately solitary orgasms.

Revenge porn

"When my daughter was 17 she let her 19-year-old
boyfriend take pictures of her naked. He apparently said
it was so he'd be able to see her whenever he wanted –
he'd never show anyone. When she found out he had
shown friends she dumped him. So he uploaded all the
pictures on his Facebook page and took off the privacy
controls. Soon, she was told by horrified friends her
pictures were all over the internet, on pornographic
sites and all sorts. And there was nothing she could
do. That was a few years ago. She's still scarred by the
experience."

Lou, father of 22-year-old daughter

Pornography tends to at least start out about sex, even
though the sort of sex mostly depicted on the internet is not
about relationships, mutual affection or shared pleasure but
frequently about purely quick, goal-oriented male satisfaction. Revenge porn is an entirely different proposition. In
revenge porn, material with sexual content is uploaded on
social media or websites but it's done with the intention of
causing maximum embarrassment, harassment and harm
to the person shown. It's not about sex but humiliation and
hate and misogyny – in most cases the person so shamed is
female although men have been attacked as well. Attack-
ing those who originally broadcast the material or those
who post it on, either with appeals to stop or with angry
exchanges, can backfire – revenge porn uploaders do it
because they enjoy the pain and humiliation caused, and
enjoy being abusive about it even more. Revenge porn is now
illegal in England and Wales. Anyone who distributes without consent a private sexual photograph or film of someone
"engaged in sexual activity or depicted in a sexual way or
with their genitals exposed where what is shown would not
usually be seen in public", will now be tried in a crown court
and could face up to two years in prison. However, it is difficult, once content has 'gone viral' and is on many websites or
in many feeds, to stop it. Images can proliferate to hundreds
of sites, with thousands if not millions of hits.

Body image

"Nothing tastes as good as skinny feels."

Model Kate Moss

Parents frequently told of their concerns about their children's feelings about their own bodies – that they were too fat, too hairy (girls) or not hairy enough (boys), the wrong shape, the wrong size. Women's size and shape in developed countries has been changing and increasing over the past 20 years. Yet at the same time the cultural ideal has been steadily decreasing. What we think we should look like has no basis in physical and emotional health, yet many women's anxiety about their bodies and dissatisfaction with their appearance leads to stress, depression and ill-health. The media has always played a role in this, displaying celebrities and role models who have unrealistic body shapes and encouraging young people to feel they have to conform or be unacceptable. Social media and constant connection with images has led to a considerable pressure on young people, and now even young children, to diet and sometimes go to extreme measures to be what they assume is 'normal'.

Harmful content

One of the truly frightening and possibly little known aspects of the internet are the websites and discussion forums that glorify and encourage self-destructive and dangerous behaviour such as self-harm, eating problems and suicide. Incitements to violence and to law or rule breaking are there too, but are almost mainstream. The sites that should particularly worry parents are the pro-self-harm sites, and the pro-ana or pro-mia ones. These provide encouragement to those with the eating disorders anorexia and bulimia, claiming it is a lifestyle choice not an illness. Doctors recognise anorexia nervosa as a serious illness, with some research suggesting anorexia nervosa has the highest rate of mortality of any psychological disorder. All these sites give tips on how to do it and how to hide it from parents. They allow vulnerable young people with problems to validate such behaviour as a coping mechanism and part of their identity with themselves as part of a supportive community that encourages such behaviour.

Grooming

Grooming is a serious problem on the internet, and can be both sexual and political. Grooming is when someone befriends and establishes an emotional connection and trust with someone, usually a young person. Face-to-face, grooming can also involve the family or other trusted adults so that they give permission to the groomer to have access to the child, or give the child confidence that the groomer is bona fide. Online, groomers often pose as people the same age as the young person or a little older – a boy or girlfriend who likes the same things or is interested in the young person. After all, in cyberspace, no-one can see you. Grooming often takes place in chat rooms or on social media sites that allow anonymous chat. Groomers will join open Facebook pages and may ask to be 'friends' with people they see contributing. Grooming is a gradual process where the young person's confidence is gained and their inhibitions lowered. If the goal is sexual, where the majority of victims will be girls, the groomer will eventually turn the discussion to sexual matters, which will become more and more explicit, and will ask to meet in person, or ask for intimate pictures to be sent. Political grooming follows much the same format but the goal may be to ask victims – male and female – to be involved in whatever activity the groomer and their cause demands.

Digital footprint

"When I tried to sound a warning to my son about some of the things he's doing and accessing on the internet he just laughed at me. It's all anonymous and free, he says – what's to worry about?"

Jamie, father of a 16-year-old

There are three things that anyone using the internet needs to know, above all:

- Nothing is free.
- Nothing is anonymous.
- Everything is shared.

Looking at the three biggest corporations working in this field, you can understand what Apple and Microsoft, valued at around $400 billion, give us for our money – they sell us objects. But Google 'gives' us information, free at point of use, so how do they make their money? Simple – in exchange for their information we give them ours, to use and control. As Julian Assange has said, "It knows every page you've ever viewed even if you don't use Google. It knows every website you've ever seen – it knows you better than your mother."

Free website material is not free – you pay with your details, even if you don't sign anything. Information is gold to companies – what you look at, where you go, what you ask, who you are and what you buy. Go online to look at clothing, beauty products, sports equipment, anything, and seconds later you'll have ads for those products appearing when – seconds later – you log into social media. Ads are targeted at you – anything you've every expressed an interest in by talking about on social media or looking at on a website, or that is assumed to be relevant by your age, gender, location and other details. In effect, the internet is a giant casino designed to let you undervalue and give away your privacy and yourself.

And that also means it's possible to trace you. Companies can tell from which computer you posted. You may appear as anonymous in public, but behind the scenes your email address and other details could be accessible – certainly to police if you have posted something unacceptable. And other users can put together all sorts of bits of information you may let slip, to learn who you are and where you are. When you do those amusing and enjoyable little quizzes that your friends send you or post on Facebook do you realise you're broadcasting a stunning amount of personal information you might not want strangers to see – your mother's maiden name, your birth date, your pet's name . . . thinking about passwords or access to bank accounts, do any of those answers seem familiar? It's called data mining and it goes on all the time.

The internet is about connections. When you put something up you're not just sharing with your friends but their friends, and their friends' friends, and all the people they have some connection with. Your history is archived – do young people realise colleges and employers now search and look and may well base college or job offers on what they see on social media? And of course, it's really difficult to track down and delete all references and photographs if you suddenly realise some of it might have been inappropriate and damaging to your reputation. A YouGov poll found today's under 35s will upload 100 hours of footage of themselves on YouTube in their lifetime, and the volume is increasing 20 fold per generation. Weddings, births and nights out figure most – those nights out may well prove your undoing.

One salient and sobering story is of the so-called "Star Wars Kid". In 2002 a 15-year-old high school student living in Canada made a video of himself wielding a stick as if it were a *Star Wars* style lightsaber. He left the video in the machine, another student found it and uploaded it to the internet where it went viral, eventually attracting a billion views. He was ridiculed and bullied online and face-to-face, resulting in some time in hospital. His family eventually sued the families of the children who uploaded the video, a case that was settled out of court. He did attract support and fans and recently has used his profile to speak out about bullying, but his life was made miserable for many years. And the video is still available . . .

There is discussion at time of writing of moves to be made to make it possible for young people to be able to delete anything they later feel inappropriate, uploaded before the age of 18. The problem may be in hunting down items that have been shared, and shared, and shared.

Posting and context

"I made a comment which my friends knew was just a joke. But it got RT-ed [retweeted] and some other people in the school saw it and took it seriously and they said some stuff and before you know it, it was going around as if I was this really mean and sarcastic person when that wasn't what I meant at all. I've heard of when it really gets out of control and goes on and on, and way beyond the school. I guess I was lucky because it did die down."

Isabella, 15-year-old girl

There are two threats implicit in using social media. One is that you and your children need to understand that online communication doesn't understand context, and the internet and social media is unforgiving of stupid mistakes. Say anything that can be taken the wrong way and you may live to regret it. Adults have lost their jobs because of silly comments taken out of context – you and your children can research the stories of Justine Sacco and Lindsey Stone. But remarks made now as teenagers may return to haunt them later. Paris Brown was appointed as the first junior Police Commissioner in Kent in 2013 and almost immediately was forced to resign when tweets she posted between the ages of 14 and 16 were found, that appeared to be racist, homophobic and in favour of drugs.

The other is that before you get upset and shame or blame someone on social media, it's worth remembering that they are real people with real lives and real feelings. We may not understand the whole story or have the right end of the stick. Tailors have an excellent motto: measure twice, cut once. That is, be absolutely sure you have it right before doing anything irrevocable. Anyone using the internet and social media needs to do the same: check twice, send once.

Threats, actual and perceived

In Chapter 2 we looked at what most parents felt were their areas of anxiety when thinking about digital technology. In the last chapter we explored the similarities and the possible differences in what might be considered the real areas of concern. In this chapter we've looked at what might be considered the more serious side – the genuine threats. As we said then we need to ask ourselves whether our anxiety is because what they might encounter and what they might do is really that dangerous, or whether there are other reasons for our fears. They can search out information or discussions that we might deny them – on sexual issues, for instance, where parents may feel embarrassed and teachers say it's not in their remit. They go elsewhere because they can and because we aren't giving them what they need. We can hardly blame them for that, or feel it's their fault when they find aspects of the internet that shock and appal us, and affect them in ways none of us anticipated.

However, before we explore what we might do about the issues we really do feel need tackling, we should also consider what might be the upsides of the internet and digital technology. It's not all bad news. And that's our next chapter.

Something for you to try

Find a media story about any issues discussed in this chapter and talk it through with your family – are the conclusions made by the media justified?

5

The opportunities of the digital world

"Should we be using the internet and digital tech in school? It's a good thing, we all use it as adults for work, entertainment and to socialise so I don't see how we can tell our children it's bad . . . but we do need to teach our children about the dos and don'ts just like you would teach your child not to touch the stove, a power socket, be careful with hot mugs etc."

Tom, father of 11-year-old son

Because this is a book about helping you to manage your own and your children's digital world, we have divided it along the line of our common anxieties, the actual worries and threats and the opportunities – the last being what we are about to explore. But in many ways, the digital world is similar to the real world – in most cases, things just are. It's not that something is in itself good or bad, harmful or benign; it's how we use it. For that reason, some of the aspects you find online that can be harmful or threatening can also be exceptionally useful and helpful. It is, as the comedian used to say, "How you tell 'em." How much you understand, how much you actively engage, how much you manage and control makes all the difference. To get the positives you have to lean in – to take part and be consciously involved in both your own activity and your children's. You need to encourage, to guide and take guidance, to make use of the opportunities presented and to mitigate the damage that is also possible. Being dynamic, not passive, is a guide point for all internet activities.

We've examined the worries and threats that can be present in your children's use of digital tech. But we need to be grounded and realistic in our review of digital technology, social media and the internet. You can't take the proper measures to protect your children and yourselves from the drawbacks until you also understand the positives. Especially since there are so many, and it is of course the positives that draw them in. So let's consider how you and your children and young people make use of the digital world and look at the opportunities offered by this technology.

Keeping in touch

"We use our tablet for 'facetime' with relatives living abroad – my parents live in New Zealand and if we didn't have this, our children would almost have forgotten them by the time we see each other once a year. And the kids would have grown so much in the gap! As it is, they chat to each other at least once a week."

Petra, mother of 10- and 15-year-old daughters

One of the very positive aspects highlighted by many respondents to our survey was the ability to keep in touch with family and friends, both over a distance and closer to home. This may be particularly vital when family members such as grandparents live some distance away. Grandparents and some parents may remember how onerous it was when you wanted to stay in touch with a granny or grandpa who lived the other side of the world in 'the old days'. It took letters – few children enjoy writing letters! – or expensive phone calls. Skype and messaging makes it free and instant.

It also means parents and kids can keep in contact on a day or night out, updating each other on progress, time expected home or the need for a lift, or indeed if an emergency occurs. And some families even use it to call members to table at meal times rather than shout up the stairs.

We'll cover this in more detail in a later chapter but digital technology can above all be helpful when parents have separated and live apart, so that children can keep in daily contact with both the parent they are with and the one they are not. It can also mean children can keep in touch with grandparents who might otherwise have fallen through the cracks of a disintegrating family. Or when children live with people other than their parents and still want to keep in touch with them. We'll be exploring the uses of digital technology in families that live apart from each other in Chapter 10.

School and home

"When I was at school many years ago my 5th form did a trip to a Welsh mountain school, learning to climb and trek and stuff. It would have been right up my street and most of my friends went. I didn't and why? Because like an idiot I put the application form at the bottom of my school bag and found it a month later, a week too late. I was so grateful when I realised my son's school had dispensed with such a stupid system."

Donna, mother of 10-year-old son
and 3-year-old daughter

Digital technology has also transformed communication between schools and parents. Parents and schools should be working in partnership to help children learn. This sometimes has proved harder in the past when parents had to make efforts to contact the school, or felt the only access was at parent and teacher evenings. Schools could often only contact parents through letters via the mail or sent home with pupils – not the best way of ensuring a communication got through! You can now get the sort of routine information you might need on school websites. Those letters that tended to either be thrown away or left to languish in the school bag – telling you the weekend soccer match had been cancelled or the venue changed, or asking if you wanted to sign your child up for a holiday or keeping you up to date on a child's results or behaviour – can now arrive as emails or texts or automated voice messages or be posted on websites.

Information such as dates of holidays and inset days, closures due to bad weather and events, with the addition of school news, staff details, suggestions and ideas, all helping parents feel they are part of school life, are freely available, 24/7. Some schools whose pupils have parents living apart use text, emails or access to the website to keep both parents equally in the know. More and more schools are using texts to tell parents if children have not turned up at school – schools using this have noted a dramatic fall in truancy.

Gaming

School and home should lead on to considering the role of digital technology in the classroom, but we'll digress into gaming for a second – you'll see why.

Of course, playing games have often been seen as either trivial or dangerous. The journal *Scientific American* has criticised one game in these terms. The game? Chess:

> "A pernicious excitement to learn and play chess has spread all over the country, and numerous clubs for practicing this game have been formed in cities and villages . . . chess is a mere amusement of a very inferior character, which robs the mind of valuable time that might be devoted to nobler acquirements, while it affords no benefit whatever to the body. Chess has acquired a high reputation as being a means to discipline the mind, but persons engaged in sedentary occupations should never practice this cheerless game; they require out-door exercises – not this sort of mental gladiatorship."

That was in the issue for July 1859. Doesn't it sound exactly like the criticism you may have heard, or made, about digital gaming?

Most young people, both boys and increasingly girls, have experience of playing computer and online games. The drawbacks may be that young people get immersed and obsessed and neglect other aspects of their life. The upside is that games, unlike watching television, are active, not passive. They demand a response – thinking, reacting, finding solutions. Games require skill and expertise – and acquiring, developing and deploying those can have dramatically positive results in young people's lives. Game

Transfer Phenomena (GTP) can be interpreted as someone not being able to tell reality from fantasy, a common anxiety and complaint about young gamers. It might involve a game-experienced person assuming a real person can be controlled in the way an avatar in a game could, thinking you can click a button on a controller to influence what they or you are doing or saying. Or by one person finding themselves reaching for a search button when looking for another in a crowd, or by looking for instantaneous satisfaction in everything you do. But a positive example might be someone in a difficult situation, possibly facing conflict, imagining a menu of options they might choose, which is far better than losing your temper or feeling powerless.

One-person games help develop the ability to find solutions and can raise self-esteem and confidence. The gamer begins to see themselves as a problem solver who is competent and capable rather than someone who can't do anything. Collaborative games can be even better because as well as allowing individual growth they engage young people in learning to cooperate. Games, whether one-person, two-person or multiple person, reward persistence and give children a real sense of achievement and development.

In gaming you learn that you have to focus and practise and go up against challenges to gain skills. You get to fail – a really vital experience. The frustration and impatience felt by a child when first playing gives way to what we want our children to have – grit and resilience as they find if they try harder, maybe try different approaches, they can succeed. Playing roleplay games can also train empathy and do what all teens have to do – try out persona and decide who they want to be. The anxiety may be that when a child plays being a psychotic murderer, a torturer, a dictator, those are the attributes they will take over into real life. The fact that very few gamers do display such behaviour suggests by following plot lines, understanding motives and living the consequences of your decisions, this allows them to imagine how it would be, accept catharsis and choose to be different.

Gaming also enhances sensory–motor coordination and mental agility. Games can give you a sense of achievement and progression. Previous generations might have achieved the same thing by endlessly practising with a yoyo or hula hoop or basketball. Playing a game might appear to have as little practical application in the real world, but is that true? Building a city that works, bringing together a fighting crew that wins the war or finds the treasure, can do as much in making you feel in control and with something to show off to those who understand. But it also develops some transferable skills – planning, organising, budgeting, concentrating. And games usually involve feedback, which the real world often does not. It can also be soothing – some games induce a form of quiet meditation that can make a bad day, an argument with a friend or an upset with someone you love, go away.

Some jobseekers are now including experience of games such as *World of Warcraft* on their CVs. Fantasy roleplaying games require you to work in unison, be organised and goal oriented. You need to communicate, delegate and systematise. You kill the monsters and acquire the treasure better if you're enthusiastic, friendly, encouraging, polite and efficient. Very few jobs now require people to work alone – most necessitate, to a lesser or greater extent, having to be part of a team. Playing games can be a team-building exercise, but less sweaty and muddy than many of the traditional types. Some employers now recognise that.

Gaming can be a source of income as well as skills. International teams of video gamers now compete at multimillion pound tournaments. Professionals can earn salaries and prize money to play in public with audiences of enthusiasts, watching while present or online. They can also earn by uploading videos of themselves playing, often with their own running commentaries and remarks – some not only lively and informative but very funny. As devotees will point out, is there that much difference watching someone play tennis or football or any other sport? It's all a demonstration of hard-earned skill that might inspire the viewer to try their own hand.

Education

"My son's primary school teachers were totally against using tablets and phones in school. So it took some getting used to when he went to secondary school and the head says he can't see the point of banning them – we have to harness them."

Gita, mother of 13-year-old son

So, back to education, where many schools and teachers are now using the myriad opportunities found in digital technology and the online world to open up education. Change in how education is carried out is nothing new – pencils and fountain pens superseded quill pens, ballpoints followed and blackboards gave way to whiteboards. Children no longer sit in lines behind desks, working on their own. Schools employ a variety of arrangements that vary from in pairs or groups around tables, to circles, to around workstations and computers. Most schools have moved from education being about teachers as experts imparting their knowledge to pupils as recipients, to teachers as guides and facilitators of children learning how to themselves acquire knowledge and use it. All schools use digital technology in some form or other now. This can range from IT lessons in which they might not only learn to use a device but to code and program too, to schools that provide every pupil with their own tablet that they are expected to use in school and take home as well. Digital technology in these situations may be used across the school in all subjects.

There are many arguments in favour of computer use. One is that students with reading difficulties such as dyslexia find computer use aids them in their learning. Another is the sheer practicality and common sense – they use them at home, will use them when they go out to work so need to develop such skills as much and as soon as possible. Yet another is that digitalised learning can be personalised, giving pupils the level of challenge or of support they need. E-books can allow schools to have updated resources for each pupil, and go behind the printed text with videos and links. Yes, students given a tablet may forget them, break them, let them run down in the middle of the lesson. But you can't claim the dog ate their homework when it was supposed to have been emailed or uploaded for the teacher to access.

Using digital technology should encourage collaborative learning. The ease of communication between pupils and teacher, pupils and pupils, means that classes can share ideas and resources easily. They can get quick feedback on their work instead of handing in paper assignments to be marked and returned often days later when they might have forgotten what they did. They will even be able to participate in live e-debates for homework. Some schools use Education City, a site where children can play educational games online. Children access from home and they think they're simply playing with their friends. What they are actually doing is their maths homework.

A study from the National Literacy Trust and Pearson suggested that touch-screen computers were particularly useful in helping boys and pupils from less well-off families to learn to read. Children in lower income households were particularly likely to read on touch-screen computers rather than printed books. There is also evidence that when pupils take home tablet computers it increases the involvement of families, so helping to motivate pupils who might otherwise be disengaged.

Digital devices can – and should – be used in classrooms to unlock pupils' potential, release creativity, sustain interest and provide intellectual challenge. Computers can support meaningful learning by:

- reducing time spent on mechanical tasks such as rewriting, producing graphs and tables
- helping find information
- helping organise information
- making it easier to share information and ideas with others

Of course, it needs teachers who are enthusiastic, proficient and familiar with the technology and possessing the skills. This is without doubt the most important aspect of using digital tech – that teachers are enthusiastic and knowledgeable. If they are, some of the ways pupils can be encouraged might be as follows:

- Having the opportunity to listen to poems and plays read by well-known performers, and being encouraged to write, record and share their own compositions.

- Having access to fully searchable digital Ordnance Survey (OS) maps of Great Britain to open up geography lessons, and historical OS maps to see how landscapes have changed over the past 120 years.
- Learning about the periodic table by viewing rotatable 3D images of the elements, together with a huge amount of detailed information.
- Having teachers assign, collect and review pupils' work, then provide detailed feedback, either individually or collectively, using annotations, text notes and voice notes directly on to pupils' documents.
- Companies, such as The Royal Shakespeare Company, offer access to free broadcasts of plays and to online resources for teachers and students.

Flipping the classroom

In traditional teaching the teacher is the focus of the classroom, giving information and instruction. The classroom tends to be the place where pupils are given and gather knowledge, and homework is where they work on that. Homework is usually expected and assumed to be the sole work of the pupil though in reality parents help and so do friends. Child-centred ideas have gradually changed education so that for some time it's been much more about young people not only researching and finding out for themselves, but also collaborating in the work that ensues. Digital technology has not just helped that – in many cases it has made that possible. Flipping the Classroom extends that journey. And if you're interested in learning more, there is plenty of research online – simply 'google' Flipped Classroom.

In the Flipped Classroom model what is intended is that teachers and pupils work in a mutually collaborative way. They try to get away from the authoritarian 'teacher knows best' framework where teachers are in charge and pupils are passive. Knowledge acquisition is what happens at home, rather than in the classroom. Pupils are asked to watch videos and podcasts prepared or sourced by the teacher, research online and discuss with each other and possibly other sources, via digital technology. In class they explore topics at greater length and depth, with greater creativity. Young people can work in groups on different projects or at different levels, gaining and using problem-solving skills. One major advantage of flipping is that each pupil can proceed at their own pace, working on subjects until they have grasped that particular aspect before moving on.

In traditional teaching the class has a fixed time on a subject or aspect of a subject – such as, in history, the dissolution of the monasteries under Henry VIII – before all having to move on together. If someone hasn't grasped the essentials, they fall behind and can become frustrated, alienated and disengaged. Flipping the Classroom means each person can return to the subject until they get it, and have their competence and capability rewarded. Schools that have successfully introduced the Flipped method have had significant advances in pupil attainment, and engagement of previously disengaged students. But it does need both school and teachers to be fully committed and prepared. Using digital technology means that in many schools in the UK today although they may not be working to the whole Flipped Classroom model, they have changed the way children work. Being able to use technology means that children can collaborate more, work to their own level more and be more creative. And in many cases, be more engaged.

Learning where access to school restricted

Digital technology has the power to transform access to education in situations where for some reason a child cannot attend a conventional school, or has to be at home for a period. This could be for instance, where a child has disabilities or is ill. Or where he or she is living in an unsafe environment, where war or community violence or religious restrictions make going to school risky or impossible. It can mean that days when school has to be shut, for inset days or bad weather or other reasons, do not have to mean pupils lose out on their education but can continue almost as if they has been in the classroom.

Gamification

"I was quite against games until my older son's teacher suggested he would actually benefit from playing *Minecraft*. They now use it in class and he was so very, very right. My son is borderline Asperger's and can be shy and quiet. He's come out of himself in school now because he's an acknowledged master at it."

Cammie, mother of sons of 11 and 14

Teachers can also use the strategy used in games to enthuse pupils. The gamification of learning is an educational approach to motivate students to learn by using video game design and game elements in learning environments. The goal is to maximise enjoyment and engagement through capturing the interest of learners and inspiring them to continue learning. Games use badges, points, levels, leader boards and challenges to inspire and encourage. Games use frequent reward to drive users on to continue to strive for excellence. Instead of waiting for homework, or a weekly, monthly or end of term test, teachers using gamification can make sure pupils see their best efforts acknowledged and rewarded as they go along. Anyone who has watched kids play video games together has seen this trend. They may be in competition but they give each other tips and advice, they share tricks. They teach each other to understand the games' systems. Gaming inherently involves systems-thinking which is best taught through collaborative learning. Using the same forms of encouragement, teachers can encourage young people to do their best.

Tweeting it

"Is it ok I've read ovr 10 bks since start of school yr? I somtimz wondr if it was wis 4 my parents 2 get me a kindle 4 xmas."

Tweet from school student in
Twitter discussion on reading and books

Using Twitter with a hashtag allows a class to continue a discussion after the class ends. It also allows teachers to end a class in a very positive way, by asking students to summarise what they've been doing. Tweets are limited to 140 characters. They may need to prioritise what they feel was the main point or message of the lesson. This means tweeters must be precise, organised and sometimes witty in their utterance. For instance, the tweet put up by one pupil asked to reflect on reading Shakespeare's *Macbeth*, purporting to come from Lady Macbeth; "We need more hand soap . . . ".

Learning to be critical and analytical

"You have to be disciplined. It's great for research but you do have to teach them balance is key. You can't believe everything you read."

Ben, father of 13-year-old son and
16-year-old daughter

Having access to the internet and all that is on it can help young people – and older people too – be more critical and analytical. The key is recognising that just because you see it in print or hear it in a podcast or video doesn't mean it is true. And this, of course, is why it's so important for us to have on-going debates with our young people, at home and at school, about what they find out there.

The internet is a lawless zone. Anyone can post on social media or set up a website. The internet is awash with 'information' from people who passionately believe what they are saying but can't always back it up with evidence. And it's also rife with misinformation, mistruths and downright lies. It does, as one parent, Timna, with a 15-year-old daughter said, "offer so much to them from what I had, as far as study and homework". But in accessing that wide range of facts and opinions we need to look for attribution, and understand it, and teach our children to do so too. As Timna said: "We were looking at information about vaccinations because my sister has a new baby. Oh my goodness, the nonsense we found by so-called anti-vaxxers! Yet people believe this stuff, because it's on the internet. We found enough by recognised medical sources to tell us it was a tissue of nonsense, thank goodness."

Gradually schools are realising Media Literacy is vital. This means being able to think critically about what you see or read, and assess whether it might be the whole truth or truth at all. A headline, for instance, may be a cut-down version that by leaving out certain facts ends up being entirely inaccurate. Among other things, Media Literacy is about:

- assessing credibility
- using different sources of information
- understanding the concept of audience manipulation
- recognising the power of advertising
- understanding the influence of commercial interest by internet providers
- learning how to stay safe online

We'll have more to say about the importance of media literacy in the final chapter.

There is evidence that many young people have already taken the message about being careful and protective. Mark Zuckerberg, founder of Facebook, said in 2010 that privacy was no longer the social norm. Teenagers can have more relaxed attitudes than their elders to what constitutes 'privacy'. However, many go to great lengths to use social media but still maintain a screen – using privacy settings, multiple accounts and fuzzy posts known as 'vague-booking' to keep their business their own. Vague-booking means making a general statement about what is happening in their life such as "Oh dear – bad day!" Real friends get in touch and ask what's happening, when they will share whatever it is with them. More distant 'friends' don't ask, or ask and are ignored.

Development of social and communication skills and thus friendships

"The internet offers opportunities for learning and positive social experiences, especially for neuro diverse individuals. You are able to find people with similar interests worldwide and communicate with them in ways that were not possible before. Obviously there are

dangers and children need guidance and age-appropriate
limits on access but overall I am all for it."

Parent with a son of 15 on the autistic spectrum

It's very easy to get the impression that the internet and
social media is all about porn, cyberbullying, misery and
mayhem. It's a similar position to that of parents who keep
their children in, fearing that the outside world has a pae-
dophile behind every bush and untold dangers lurking. In
fact, just as the real world dangers have been blown out of
all proportion, online dangers have also been exaggerated.
And for the same reason. The media has no interest in print-
ing stories that say "Teenagers have a wonderful time connecting with friends" or "Children learn so much from new
technology". Bad news is what sells and bad news is what is
always disseminated.

Using social media can in fact aid children and young
people in developing social skills. A shy child who might
need time to think of an answer, gets it in the delay between
thought and keyboard. Finding friends online can be trans-
lated into being friends offline. Or, into an increase in skills
and confidence that allows them to make new friends in
their offline community or developing old connections. Social
media can allow young people to try, fail and try again and to
gradually learn what works in making and keeping friendships. A young person who has a particular interest that is
not shared by anyone they know around them can find a community online that can echo their passion and reinforce their
pursuit. And groups of friends can extend and develop their
relationships outside school even when they live some distance away from each other. In a group of young people face-
to-face the loudest and most confident can monopolise the
conversation giving little space for the quieter ones. Online,
everyone can have their say and that may allow some kids
to come to the fore who might otherwise have always been
in the shade.

Another parent also with a son with autism said:

"He struggled at primary school but it really went
downhill at secondary and in spite of the fact he is really

intelligent they told me to give up on any idea of his going to university. Then I got him onto the internet, and he was lucky enough to get a far more enlightened teacher. He made internet friends with his passion for politics and then a few guys at school started to understand him. He's doing a Masters degree now and has a wide circle of both internet and real world friends. I honestly don't think any of this would have been possible in my day, pre-internet. It was a life saver."

Opportunities for creativity

"My son likes making videos and publishing them on YouTube. I'm just in total awe at what he seems to find so easy to do. I could never approach anything like that when I was his age – I couldn't now!"

Jamie, father of 16-year-old son

What the internet and digital technology allows for, above all things perhaps, is the opportunity to be creative. Young people have always wanted to be makers – to be authors, poets, singers and songwriters and lately to be photographers and film makers. That used to mean writing a diary, strumming on a guitar or using your parents' cine camera. Young people can now progress from halting personal blogs to publishable material, on their computers. They can go from tinkering around with a few chords to having learnt how to play instruments via apps, and to composing music of all sorts. They can produce professional looking films and videos and take and edit photographs. All of this and more can be uploaded into the public sphere, to be consumed and judged and in some cases to be seen and approved not just locally but nationally and worldwide. And, of course, be purchased or attract funding or other perks. Popular videos on YouTube attract advertising and firms will offer money or goods to bloggers and vloggers who feature their products.

The internet has the potential to open up worlds to young people. It puts them in touch with other people and ideas, and gives them access to things they can do for fun.

It can also lead them into career possibilities – things their parents may never have thought about or be able to do.

Access to community, and role models

"I was talking about an author I particularly love the other day and my daughter persuaded me to look at his website and then go to his Facebook page. I'm not a fan mail person but it was so easy to just 'like' something he'd said and add that I loved his books and thank you for them. I couldn't believe it – I got a lovely message from him an hour later!"

Sammi, mother of 16-year-old daughter

The internet is full of under 30-year-olds who not only entertain our young people but are role models to them, often extremely inspiring ones. They write content, create animations and make and upload videos of themselves. For instance, some film themselves playing games online, laughing and swearing through running commentaries of their gaming. Others offer chat about their lives, make up and style tips, shopping advice and constant smiles and fun. Some share their worries and lack of self-confidence and panic attacks, and these can attract millions of views and comments from teenagers thanking them for sharing.

There are countless others whose talents range from undeniable expertise in directing and making videos or singing or knowing how to mix chat about serious issues such as education, homophobia and healthcare with the trivia of pop culture, to simply being cool and attractive.

But what is noticeable is that all the vloggers are 'ordinary'. Attractive, but not the sort of unachievable and unrealistic looks peddled by the fashion and film industries. Vloggers made the 'big butt' fashion popular. It may then have been taken over and brought to unrealistic levels by some pop stars but it began as no more than "So my backside looks big in this? Who cares? And actually I like it – don't you?" And their lives seem ordinary too – mucking around with friends, chatting inconsequentially, joking, shopping. They tend to be clean cut, clean living and, above all, kind.

The sort of person, in fact, you'd like your teenager to be and to befriend. Even the ones who make jokes about drug taking and rebellious behaviour do so tongue in cheek. Teenagers see them as the best friends they want and may not have. They set out simply to do what they liked and connect with others. That they have ended up making a very good living from it is accidental, but telling. And it does form a cheering undercurrent to some of the nastiness that does exist on social media with some people happy to 'troll' – be unpleasant to others. The more our teenagers see that niceness isn't just heart-warming but actually pays, the better.

The unique and new aspect of YouTube stars is that the relationship between them and their audience is real. Consider the old-style Hollywood stars who were remote and untouchable. Fans were invited to love and emulate, but at a distance, and with knowledge that you were very unlikely to ever actually meet them or be like them. These new role models aren't celebrities with celebrity lifestyles – their appeal lies in their being willing to come from behind the screen. This is not just in what they do and talk about but in the two-way nature of the relationship. They talk, the audience can ask, and they answer. Often almost immediately. It really is a conversation.

Identity development and increase in competence, confidence and self-esteem

> "I have noticed that since I allowed my older son to have a social media page he's come out of his shell and is far more willing – and able! – to put a point of view."
>
> Ben, father of 13-year-old son and 16-year-old daughter

What all teenagers spend much of their adolescence doing is working on their identity. Who am I, what do I want to be, where am I going? They try on variations of their personality at the same time as trying out different clothes, music, ideas. The crazy styles may get up the nose of and sometimes alarm their parents – that's partly what they're designed to do – but mostly it's about seeking their self. They want to feel right, they want to know they can deliver, they want to feel capable. This is why they can be so touchy about any suggestion that they are still children and need to be looked after – even though, to a certain extent, they still are. One of the big positives of the internet is that a lot of this experimentation can take place safely behind a screen and even anonymously. They can espouse causes and not have to march in the streets to do so. They can make political statements that may be extreme and know they can withdraw without their cover having been blown when they change their mind. And increasingly they can put their name to what they believe and how they feel and know they will find fellow thinkers. Slowly and carefully they can practise putting forward their views, so that when they are in a face-to-face situation they can have the confidence to voice them.

The sensible generation

A significant number of risky behaviours associated with young people have dropped over the last 15 years. Smoking, drinking, taking drugs and getting pregnant have all reduced. Thus there has been a 25% reduction in smoking among 11–15-year-olds since the year 2000, and an even more marked reduction in drinking. Figures show that among this age group the numbers drinking alcohol at least once a week fell from 50% in 2002 to 23% in 2014. The same pattern can be seen in the use of illegal drugs, and teenage conception rates are now at their lowest since the 1960s. This information can be found in *Key Data on Adolescence 2015*, which is published by the Association for Young People's Health (www.youngpeopleshealth.org.uk).

Of course we should not be complacent – we still have one of the highest teenage pregnancy rates in Europe. And, there is concern that other behaviours may reflect the stresses experienced by this age group, for example through self-harm or eating disorders.

The Sensible Generation may have come about because of the internet. Smoking, drug taking, joy riding and drinking may all arise because bored teenagers, with nowhere to go and nothing to do, hung around on street corners and drifted into such behaviours. Teenage pregnancy is far more likely to happen when drink or drugs are involved. Now, instead of being bored or even being on a street corner they are in contact with each other and being entertained online. We may have swapped all those behaviours that were a health hazard with others – obesity, lack of exercise and an inability to manage real-world social connection. The challenge for parents is to cherry pick – take the advantages offered in digital technology, social media and the internet and mitigate the disadvantages – about that, more later.

First steps into romantic relationships in safety

"I can't see the problem with sex on the internet. I use a few places to put me in touch with boys. Yes, the talk can get raunchy. So what? If I don't like what they're saying or asking I just navigate away and block them."

16-year-old girl

As we've already mentioned, the rates of teenage pregnancy in the UK have reduced over the last 15 years. You can't get pregnant or catch STI from screen sex and can explore both sexuality and sex a safe screen away. Users can get in touch with each other and either discuss behaviour, tastes or beliefs, or actually act out sexual contact. But if it gets too hot or intrusive, you can simply click away and block the other person from future contact. Relationships may start early – 13, 14 is not uncommon – but can be short term and uncomplicated. It's a lot better than waiting till 17, having a torrid sexual affair that crashes and burns with total heartache and the after-effects of pregnancy or infections. By the time they are ready for real relationships, today's teens may have far more experience in running a relationship than their parents ever did. And because they may then invest less emotional intensity, they can emerge with less emotional damage. But it can also mean real relationships are hard to manage – you have little experience at genuine intimacy even though you might be used to disclosing an awful lot about yourself, on screen.

Opportunities for discussion and boundary setting

"It was my fault we hadn't talked about sex, I was
too shy. When we found out he'd been having torrid
discussions online with a variety of other boys we finally
got down to what we should have done ages before –
talking about the fact he's gay, and discussing sex and
safe sex and everything. My brother is gay and he didn't
come out until he was in his 20s, and was miserable.
So I have to be grateful that we were pushed into it far
earlier."

Mother of 14-year-old son

What digital technology can offer is an ideal focus for having
in-depth discussions with children and young people about
risks, desired behaviour and boundaries. Discussion on how
you use your device and what you do when on it can be an
extension of issues you may have been explaining from the
time your baby began to crawl. Be nice, be kind, be careful, be
safe. From a very early age parents know part of their job –
after loving, caring for and nourishing a child – is to socialise
the individual. We teach them to say please and thank you
and not to hit little brothers or sisters, or friends. When we
hand over the first piece of digital technology, we need to be
aware that it's not just about teaching them the particular
game (or letting them play around while we get on with making dinner), it has to be about setting the guidelines. Again,
more of that later but here it's worth saying that rather than
seeing this as a chore or a battle, we need to see it as an
opportunity. Because in setting boundaries around technology use, we can also review and consider the need for boundaries at all; we can think about what we want to say to them,
what we want to teach them and what we need to discuss so
that those boundaries are appropriate and effective.

Opportunities to make a difference

Young people have always wanted to make a difference.
Many – 80% of 16–24-year-olds in a recent UK survey – have
done voluntary work in the previous year. In past generations

they might have marched – some still do – or signed petitions, but with a certain amount of scepticism that it would make any difference. Social media and the internet have dramatically changed that. Petition sites such as 38 Degrees and Change.org can be used to set up any petition, while social media can spread the word. People can see how highlighting injustice or asking for change can be effective, in small and large ways. Online campaigns often rely on memes to make this possible.

A meme is an idea or information package that can act as a virus – it can spread with surprising speed and reach. We call it 'going viral', when an initial challenge, plea or alert suddenly seems to be everywhere.

Some viral campaigns simply ask people to recognise a situation and sign a petition to change it. Having women on UK banknotes, honouring Sir Nicolas Winton (who rescued so many children from the Nazis) with a stamp, saving many women, activists, journalists from prison or death. Others ask participants to do something, to spread the word in addition to donating or raising funds.

The Ice Bucket Challenge was possibly one of the most famous. The Ice Bucket Challenge focused attention on charities supporting ALS, known in the UK as Muscular Dystrophy. Participants were challenged to make and upload a video of themselves being drenched with a bucket filled with ice and water, and then issuing a dare to two other people to do the same. They were also meant to donate to ALS or Muscular Dystrophy research, and publicise this cause. Politicians, internet figures, music, sporting and film stars, as well as millions of ordinary people, did the challenge. It raised millions for these charities in the US and UK, but, more importantly, going on internet searches, massively raised awareness of motor neurone disease.

Check One Two was a campaign started by two young men inspired by Wendy Gough whose son had died of testicular cancer. Too shy to see his doctor about his symptoms, by the time he did seek help it was too late. His mother dedicated herself to educating schoolboys about the disease, and brothers Simon and Andrew Salter decided to take it to another level. To raise awareness of testicular cancer they asked well-known men – and any men who would do so! – to take and upload pictures of themselves clutching their genitals, with the hashtag 'Feeling Nuts'. The reaction was a perfect example of the different standpoints of the generations. Kids thought it was hilarious and took the message. Some – I stress only some – older people thought it was "nothing short of the worst sort of puerile indecency if not obscenity – utter filth that people of decency and even schoolboys would recoil from" (clearly someone who has no idea what schoolboys would recoil from . . .); "That youth indulges in vulgarity does not make it acceptable in civilised society." (Letters in *The Times*). #Feelingnuts however does seem to have ended the embarrassed silence around testicular cancer – millions have checked out the website and taken part in the challenge. The website offers, among other things, to allow you to "set a calendar alert to remind you to check your wang danglers".

Some internet memes are simply 'feel good'. Choirs, orchestras and individuals certainly used to go out and play in their community, spreading cheer and an appreciation of classical music or dance. And of course groups of people got together to do amateur productions. Being able to upload a video of the event has meant many more do so now, and their surprise performances can be enjoyed by a larger audience. YouTube is full of 'Random Acts of Culture' and "Flash Mob' performances that attract millions of views.

Many memes are silly and dangerous, and we've discussed these earlier. It's worth noting that the dangerous ones are often self-limiting – users soon move on to the next, which is just as likely to be harmless if not helpful. But most are some simply fun and quite a few are inspired, entertaining and uplifting.

Access to support

If the internet allows harmful memes and disinformation to spread and can encourage spiteful and harmful behaviour it also provides access to so much help and support – far, far more than was ever accessible before. Teenagers can now via a few clicks find reassuring and helpful information about anything that worries them. Health questions (what could that lump be and should I ask for advice about it?), emotional questions (what do I do about bullying, or my family arguments?), questions about sexuality, eating problems, appearance, friendships. Sites can be specific – such as www.bullying.co.uk for advice on bullying or www.b-eat.co.uk for advice on eating disorders. Or general such as www.thesite.org for teenagers and young people, covering your body, mental health, drugs, money . . . anything! Most can not only give reassuring information, they can put the young person in contact with online, phone or face-to-face professional help – someone to talk to or someone to go further in dealing with whatever issue it is.

Social media also gives more young people more helpful attention than unhelpful, and access to support from their peers. Because of the prominence in news stories of trolling or bullying happening online, we tend to be less aware that often young people pose a question or make a remark and get exactly what they want – affirmation by other users, and often helpful suggestions. A 'like' to a post, or a comment that agrees or shares similar experiences, can have enormously positive effects on those involved. Research suggests that both posting and getting responses on social media can trigger the production of feel-good hormones that satisfy and comfort users, and encourage them to continue the activities. We like talking about ourselves – it makes us feel validated and 'real'. Knowing others are listening can be reassuring. It strengthens relationships and promotes new ones.

Go forth . . .

The internet is a bit like a bicycle. It's neither good nor bad. It can lead you into terrible danger, if you misuse it to ride on motorways and swerve in front of cars. Or, it can get and keep you fit and allow you to travel to the most beautiful and useful places. The task and challenge for parents is to manage digital technology and the internet. Understanding the risks and appreciating the possibilities is the key. We need to learn how to negotiate our own use for it to be helpful not harmful, and to pass these skills on to our young people.

In the next chapter we will be exploring child development and how this relates to your child's interests in digital technology, and how understanding what is going on helps us to help them be safe.

Something for you to try

Sit down on your own or with a friend or your partner and discuss how much you talked with your child/young person about the positives and opportunities of digital use, and how much about the threats. Come up with an approximate ratio – 1 to 1? 10 anxieties to every positive? You say!

Now sit down with your children/young people and ask them how much you talked with them about the positives and opportunities of digital use, and how much about the threats. Let them come up with an approximate ratio – 1 to 1? 10 anxieties to every positive? Listen to what they say!

6

Child development and technology

"I'm a nursery nurse and one of my colleagues drew my attention recently to a worrying trend. She noticed one child who always looked down at first when you spoke to him, as if when he heard a voice he expected it to come from something in his hands. We realised he's not the only one, and it's the kids whose parents think iPads and apps on their phones are the answer to a crying child."

Sandra, mother of two teenagers
and a child care professional

As we've seen in previous chapters, some of the anxieties that parents and professionals have voiced relate to the way digital technology may affect children and young people's development. Parents said they were concerned young and growing children spent too long gaming and could become addicted. Or that they felt long hours inside on a screen were replacing healthy activities, and that their children might be losing out on real friendships by finding it easier to connect via the internet than face-to-face. Some physiologists and health professionals have voiced fears that child and adolescent development and both emotional and physical well-being may be adversely affected by long hours using screens, and fewer hours being physically active or interacting with real people in the real world.

However, few parents can deny that a screen, whatever it might be showing, can often be the answer to a prayer. If your youngster is quietly watching a children's programme they're unlikely to be running around risking life and limb, breaking up the happy home or fighting with a sibling. Meanwhile, in the peace and quiet you can get on with making a meal or whatever else you need or want to do. Children watching television has given way to babies watching and manipulating tablets and children of all ages working on laptops, tablets or mobile phones – all in the apparent relative safety of your own home.

The availability of digital technology has had profound effects on everyone, no matter what age they are. From the first years of life the use of this technology can influence physical development such as hand–eye coordination. It may also influence the way thinking, language and learning change and develop. Perhaps even more importantly it has the potential to impact on social development.

Yet the influence of the digital does not just go one way. The child's interests and personality will affect the way he or she makes use of this technology. Some will be fascinated by everything digital, while others will remain more interested in traditional toys and books. On top of this the way parents and other members of the family use technology will have an important influence on the child. The child can be encouraged or discouraged, helped or hindered in exploring the digital world. Friends and the wider social group will also have a part to play. If your son or daughter sees other children using tablets, signing up for social media websites, sending photos on a new app, then clearly that influence will be a powerful factor in the way the digital world is understood.

In this chapter we will first outline some of the main factors influencing child development. As the child grows older he or she gradually changes, showing new skills and abilities. All parents want to know what to expect at different ages. However it is difficult to give firm ages for many skills and abilities. Even walking and talking do not occur at exactly the same age in every child. Many factors influence the timetable of events, including genes, temperament, parenting, the family environment and so on. The years of childhood are best seen as a series of changes and transitions to different ways of handling situations or making sense of the world. The move from one stage to another will not be one giant leap, nor a step across a divide on a given birthday. Development is a series of steps, some minor, some major, and some more easily managed than others.

The early years of childhood are very important, but what happens then does not fix children forever. The benign effects of a happy childhood can be undermined by later stressful events. However it is equally true that positive experiences at a later stage can do a lot to overcome the impact of a troubled childhood.

Physical development

The development of very young children is full of highly visible milestones as far as physical development is concerned. These include crawling, walking, running, climbing stairs, and so on. As children grow they learn new skills, often through play or exercise. Of course parents do worry about whether their son or daughter is developing at the same rate as other children. Where some aspect of development appears to be slower than expected, it is important to get advice from a GP, a health visitor or other professional person. There are many different reasons why change and growth in one area may not be happening, and exploring the amount of time spent on digital media may be just one of the issues that you might need to consider. It may be that a developmental assessment is necessary to identify where some extra help is needed. On the other hand the professional may be able to provide reassurance that the apparent delay is well within the normal range. In all cases good information about child development in the early years will be of great help to families. The more good information is available, the better.

In later childhood many new physical skills will develop. Better coordination will allow the child to learn to ride a bike, play ball games, take part in playground activities, and engage in team sports. All the evidence shows that exercise during childhood is of great importance for future health. However with the restriction on PE in schools, and the loss of many schools' sports grounds, it is even more important that parents and other carers find opportunities for children to exercise regularly.

Anxiety over child safety has an important effect on exercise levels during childhood. Such fears have led to more and more children being taken to school in the car, reducing opportunities for daily exercise, and giving children the message that "it's dangerous out there". Many schools have tried various ways to address this, with safe cycle paths being created, group "walk to school" projects and attempts to bar parents from parking even for a drop-off near the school gates. All this is of course of great value, and to be encouraged where possible. Some schools are now insisting their pupils run a mile each morning before lessons, and report a significant improvement in health and well-being.

But what about the digital devices – do they impact on physical development? There is wide public anxiety about the effects of too much screen time. Many hours spent in front of a screen will of course reduce the amount of exercise the child is getting. It is certainly likely that lowered levels of exercise, combined with certain eating habits, will affect weight. Evidence shows that the number of children in the UK who are overweight or obese has increased markedly in the last two decades. This is of serious concern. We cannot say that there is a direct link between obesity and the amount of time the child sits in front of a screen. However we can say that lowered levels of exercise combined with high levels of screen time is not good for child development.

But is it all bad news? Young children may be developing hand–eye coordination by moving icons around on a screen, or by finding ways of touching, poking or shaking their device so that the image or the screen changes colour or plays a favourite tune. And once on their feet and mobile, what they see and do on screen can be used to motivate them to become physically active. For instance, the result of that touching, poking or shaking can give them the prompt to jump up and either run around, spin around or turn somersaults.

Attachment

One vital area of child development has been suggested by some child psychologists as being possibly affected by early screen use and that is the area of attachment. Attachment is one of the key processes that ensure the survival of the species. Recent research on the early years has focussed particularly on brain development. These studies have shown that the formation of strong attachment bonds facilitates brain development during the first years of life. Parents connect with their babies and build bonds with 'attachment behaviours'. These would be actions such as making eye contact, cuddling, touching, playing, cooing and making sounds and talking, even though the baby at that stage cannot understand the words. They do understand tone and intention, and by responding to your baby you help the brain develop during the formative early years. On the other hand stressful early experiences, where the infant is anxious or fearful, may have the effect of inhibiting healthy brain development.

Baby and parent become mutually interdependent, each using behaviours to create close bonds. Communication, attunement and responsiveness are probably the key elements that contribute to the development of attachment in the early years. Both parent and infant engage in attachment behaviour. The baby will smile, cry, show distress or pleasure, and so on. The parent will feed, soothe, cuddle, or ignore the baby depending on the situation. The degree to which the two can read each other's signals will influence later relationships.

As an example, an important element in helping the baby make sense of the world will be the way parents respond to crying. Does the crying elicit a caring response? Does it create anxiety and fussing? Or does the baby's distress lead to being left alone to cry? Most psychologists believe that these early experiences are important building blocks in assisting the baby to build what may be called 'an internal model' of how relationships work.

These early experiences are critical in building the bond between parent and child. Once the child grows up the experiences of infancy may seem to be far in the past, but these remain the building blocks upon which later interaction is based. From the point of view of the child it is from these early experiences that a sense of trust in other people is developed. Research shows us that close physical contact, having basic needs met, the sense of being understood, having the chance to play and develop language, all these things contribute to healthy child development.

Attachment behaviours are not restricted to the early years. They may change in form or expression, but attachment is the basis for all relationships between parents and their offspring. As an example the development of trust between adult and child will have its roots in these early years. Trust will be a central theme as the child matures, where he or she will be needing the support of parents but also needing to develop independence outside the family context. Another example of how attachment experiences play out will be shown in the development of social relationships with others outside the family. The relationships that children develop with their friends and with the wider peer group will be very much influenced by the attachments experienced in the home.

But in understanding how important are those human to human interactions not only to the bond between baby and parent but also to brain development you can see how there might be anxiety over screen use. We've quoted a nursery nurse who has seen how some young children in her charge responded to a voice by expecting it to come from a screen. We don't yet know how early screen use may affect attachment and brain development, but some psychologists are concerned enough to say children younger than the age of two should not just severely limit their screen time but have none at all.

Thinking and communication

As will be obvious to all parents, the ability of the child to think, to solve problems, and to understand the world will gradually improve with age. It is often said that the child is a scientist, since he or she will be trying from the earliest moments to understand the world. The baby will do this through the senses, learning that different behaviours will elicit different responses from the parent. Smiling at the mother will in most cases elicit positive, loving responses – cuddling, cooing, tickling and bouncing – whilst crying may elicit many different responses – at best comfort and concern. Crying is a major form of communication for the infant, indicating the expression of distress.

Whilst the senses play a key role in infancy, with age the child uses other methods to explore the world. Here language is central, as the child begins to be able to ask questions. At the same time the parent is conveying information through language, whether that involves teaching about danger, encouragement to explore new realms, story-telling and so on. The gradual increase in memory capacity is another important element in the development of thinking. The more the child can memorise, the greater his or her vocabulary, and the wider the experiences he or she can draw on in the quest for understanding.

Children develop many different strategies for finding out about the world. With languages comes the capacity to ask questions. Many readers will know about the stage, usually between three and four years of age, when "Why?" becomes a favourite word. The continual repetition of this word can drive a parent to distraction, but for the child this is an essential representation of the basic curiosity that drives us all to understand the world around us. Digital devices may be not only valuable but become a child's favourite recourse. Unlike parents, a digital device is within a child's control and will respond to poking, prodding, shaking or whatever every time and never become annoyed or bored.

In the early years before schooling begins children will still show evidence of reasoning and problem-solving. However the pattern of thinking will be closely related to the immediate world around them. Even 6- and 7-year-olds will still be working primarily from what they can experience directly through their senses and because of what has happened to them. From this stage on, however, children become more able to think through ideas. They can begin to weigh up possibilities and compare different explanations for events. Their thinking will become less concrete, and they will start to understand the place of symbols. A good example is how children understand a street map. Older children will be able to see that this represents their town or city even if the cars and houses are not shown on the map.

The skills associated with abstract thinking will develop gradually at the later end of primary school and then in the first years of secondary school. This type of thinking will allow more sophisticated approaches to problem-solving, as well as the ability to carry out simple scientific experiments. In such situations the child will need to be able to imagine different alternatives and try these out systematically to be able to arrive at the right solution.

A famous experiment demonstrated the differences in thinking between 8- and 9-year-olds, and 12- and 13-year-olds. The children were presented with what is called a 'concept-formation problem'. They were shown pictures of cars and tools. Half of the cars and tools had wheels, and half did not. Whenever a picture of a car or a tool with wheels was presented, a light came on above the child's head. The task was to find out what made the light go on. Only half the younger children solved the problem, and those who did took almost all the 72 trials to come to the right solution. On the other hand all the older children solved the problem, and some did it in less than 10 trials.

The ability of the older ones to raise alternative explanations, try them out and then discard them if they were wrong, was the key. They would say things like: "It must be transportation, no, that doesn't work, I will try something else. . ." For the younger ones they seemed to become stuck on an early idea, suggested by the first set of pictures, and they would continue with this idea, even if the facts clearly contradicted this. In other words the younger children were demonstrating concrete thinking, whilst the older ones were able to use abstract thought to solve the problem.

Children's ability to communicate and to understand the communications of others is central to their development. Children gradually grow in their ability to listen and to understand what is said to them. Whether they do listen will be partly to do with their level of intellectual development, but will also partly be to do with whether they value listening to others. Many children have the experience that adults tend not to listen to them, or show respect for their views. If this is the case, children themselves will be likely to copy that model. Even good listeners will be likely to turn off if the speaker shows no interest in them.

Children will continue to increase their working vocabulary as their knowledge extends into different areas. Children are capable of using their language skills in many different ways.

Some examples might include:

- expressing an idea out loud
- putting feelings into words

- arguing a case, even at a simple level
- describing and recounting an experience to someone who was not present
- questioning to find out more about a certain topic
- offering support or sympathy
- exchanging an opinion with someone else
- disagreeing with someone during an argument

Children will vary in their confidence in relation to the use of language. How communication is used in the home will be critical in determining the child's ability to use language in all sorts of settings. The parents will be role models in this respect, as the child will be learning how others speak, how language is used, whether one person listens to another, how disagreements are worked out, and so on. Of course the school will certainly play a part, as there will be encouragement to speak in public. Examples may include taking part in discussions in class, presenting work in a public assembly, and working with others on a shared task.

The use of language is of course closely related to the use of digital devices. The wider the vocabulary of a child, the more value the child will be able to get out of the huge possibilities available on the internet. It is often the case that adults see the use of computers and other digital devices as a passive activity. They view the child as a receiver of information, the device being the medium through which information is sent through. However this is not always the case. As we have already seen, digital devices and the internet offer every imaginable possibility for being creative, for exploring the world, for obtaining new information, and for playing an active role in social interaction.

Emotional development

An essential part of the child's development is the ability to understand and manage emotions. This is something that begins very early on. As they grow through the early years, children will be expected to cry less, and to avoid uncontrollable temper tantrums when they cannot have their own way. Being able to 'delay gratification', in other words to learn to wait for rewards, is a fundamental aspect of this early maturing process. Children will need to acquire what is known as 'emotional competence'. By this we mean being able to cope appropriately with one's own and other people's feelings.

What is 'appropriate' will depend on the child's culture, age, gender and individual personality. Emotional competence is a term that covers many different skills, including:

- an awareness of one's own emotions
- an ability to recognise other people's emotions
- an ability to use a vocabulary appropriate to a variety of emotions
- the capacity for sympathy regarding other people's emotions
- an ability to recognise that inner emotional states do not necessarily appear on the outside
- the capacity for adaptive coping, rather than distress, despair and depression following challenges and upsets
- the capacity to control and manage one's feelings, and accept the full range of emotions that will be experienced in life

These elements are linked in various ways, and of course the skills involved in emotional competence will develop at a different pace for different children. Some of the skills will not appear before the child reaches the adolescent stage. But we expect even children to be able to 'monitor' emotions – to be able to regulate their intensity and duration. Thus it might be appropriate for a child to cry following a fall in the playground, but crying in this situation would not be expected to last for long. On the other hand following the death of a pet, for example, it might be quite acceptable for a child to feel sadness and grief for quite a period of time thereafter.

A child's emotions can be managed in many different ways. In the early years it is likely that the adult will play a key role here. If distress is evident the parent may soothe the child, find ways of distracting the child, or even remove him or her to different room or situation. The parent will also be expressing values about emotional expression. In some families it will be acceptable for a child to express feelings, and to be open about sadness or happiness, anger or frustration. In other families this sort of expression is not encouraged, so that the child learns to hold back from expressing feelings in public.

As the child grows older he or she begins to develop strategies to manage feelings through his or her own efforts. Of course much of this is learnt, and it is learnt mainly through observation of those in the immediate environment. Parents and siblings have an important part to play, but as soon as the child is with other children of the same age, whether in nursery or pre-school, additional learning will be taking place about how to manage feelings. Gender is also very important here. There is no doubt that there are differences between boys and girls in the expression of emotion. It seems that in our society it is less acceptable for boys to talk about their feelings. This leads to a situation where girls are more open and more skilled in expressing emotions.

It is worth noting that some emotions are more acceptable than others. It may be allowable or even encouraged for a child to say he or she feels sad or worried. An emotion like anger is seen in a different light. Children will be expected to control their angry feelings much earlier than their sad or anxious feelings. However, gender plays a part here too. Boys may be expected to 'stand up for themselves', whilst girls may be expected to avoid conflict and be conciliatory where there is conflict. As with many other aspects of development the values of society play a big role in determining how these are managed and expressed.

Finally we should mention school-based programs designed to encourage emotional intelligence. One such program that is current in many primary schools in the UK is called SEAL (social and emotional aspects of learning). Here the teacher works with the group to encourage an understanding of feelings. The program helps the children develop skills to manage their own emotions and the emotions of other people. Other programs used in school include things like Circle Time and Nurture Groups. The use of such material is important, as it encourages resilience and emotional health and well-being.

How much can children learn about emotion from the digital world? There are worries that because games can only react in limited ways, children who spend more time interacting with screens than with people may find it harder to develop the ability to understand and 'read' other people's emotions. However, increasingly emotion is very much a part of the digital world. The smiley face on your smart phone is just one example of how emotion can be conveyed through digital devices. Children and young people will be familiar with 'emoticons' or 'emojis'. These are symbols used in texting and messaging that have been developed to indicate a wide range of feelings. They are used more and more by young people to fill in that gap when you can't hear or see someone, but you need to convey feeling as well as your written word. Through digital media there are a variety of means to express emotion, and thus it is especially important that children learn to recognise, understand and manage their own feelings. It may be assumed that the use of digital devices is an intellectual activity, but the role of emotion is a significant one. We must be sure to prepare children for this aspect of the digital world. The importance of a face-to-face, human-to-human grounding in understanding emotions needs to be recognised.

Social development and the role of the peer group

As we have noted already, a significant amount of development occurs within the peer group setting. Children learn from one another, and this learning will include skills as diverse as language and communication, the management of feelings, and physical coordination. In addition the process of becoming involved in a group outside the home raises issues to do with friendship, values and attitudes, acceptance or rejection, popularity or isolation. While it may seem to some that the peer group only becomes really important during the teenage years, this is not true. Peer influence may not be quite as powerful during the primary school years, but the social arena remains a very important location for development.

From the earliest times in pre-school settings children are tackling important tasks to do with social relationships. They have to learn to understand the cues that other children send that will oil the wheels of relationships. How to play together? How to share? How to deal with another child who is cross or upset? How to control one's own feelings of hurt or distress? These are the skills that are being learnt from the early days. Where such skills are not learnt, relationships become problematic, with children experiencing the feeling of being an outsider.

The significance of friendship develops slowly over time. Before the age of five it is unlikely that a child will have a special friend, although there will certainly be playmates. These are others with whom the child enjoys playful activities. When school starts many children start to form friendships that are more significant. Here a friend may be someone with whom it is possible to:

- talk together
- share possessions and activities
- play together
- feel a sense of loyalty

As the child gets older these friendships become more stable and develop into closer relationships. The concept of 'best friend' becomes important, and such relationships will be helpful in providing support and a feeling of belonging.

Popularity becomes a significant element of social relationships, and the peer group will be dividing into different social groupings as the child progresses through primary school. At this stage friendships are likely to be single-sex relationships, primarily because the activities of boys and girls differ significantly during middle and late childhood. Where relationships break down this can be painful, and it is here that the child may learn what it is like when things go wrong between close friends. Of course some children will be more sociable than others. In addition some will be more skilful at managing relationships. Those who are popular are usually children who have some of the following characteristics:

- being alert to the emotional cues of others
- being willing to share
- being able to conciliate or mediate
- being willing to stand back some of the time, rather than wanting to be a leader at every opportunity
- having a generally stable mood

For those who find it hard to make friends, it may be that extra support from adults will be necessary. To be isolated in a group, or to be rejected by others, is an upsetting experience. Children in this situation may find that their learning is affected. The feelings associated with rejection are painful and can interfere with other aspects of life. It is often said that playgrounds can be cruel places, and parents, carers and teachers need to be alert to the needs of children who find themselves on the fringes of social groups at school.

In terms of the digital world, it will be obvious that friendship and the peer group are hugely significant here. From early on children will engage with the digital world in association with others of the same age. This may involve signing up for a website, sharing ideas about how to use a tablet, using the internet for projects at school, or starting to play games on a console or other device. Children will be influenced by what others of the same age are doing, and much of the learning about the digital world will take place within the peer group. It is for this reason that the development of social skills is so important. Children will be making use of these skills when they use digital devices. The more self-confidence they have, and the more they are aware of possible pressures from others, the more they will be able to use digital devices in a safe and sensible manner.

Something for you to try

Be alert to how other children are using digital devices. When you are out and about, make a mental note of the age of children who you see online, playing games, watching a film, or whatever it might be. Consider whether you consider this a good thing? Discuss with other close adults your attitude to the use of digital devices among young children. How young is too young, from your point of view? You should be able to have an interesting discussion about this.

7

Adolescent development and technology

The teenage years are often considered the time when parents face the greatest challenges in relation to the digital world. As we have made clear, the challenge actually starts earlier – there are certainly issues for parents to consider during childhood. Children will be showing an interest in digital devices from the time that they can talk and touch a screen. However, the gradually increasing independence that comes with the end of primary school brings with it some new and perhaps more testing situations for parents to deal with, particularly in relation to the digital world.

As children reach the age of 10 or 11 there are four things that contribute to a changed relationship with the digital world. In the first place new technical skills develop, enabling children to use a wider range of possibilities in the digital world. Secondly, this is a time when there will be a drive for increasing autonomy. Young people will be more likely to want to do things on their own, and to show that they can do things without adult help.

Thirdly, the early years of adolescence bring with them a need for privacy, so that young people will be less willing to share what they are doing with parents. And lastly at this time there will be a stronger focus on friends and the peer group. Opportunities for pursuing social relationships online become that much more important.

It is especially important to understand how adolescence is different from childhood. The more adults know about this stage of development, the easier it will be to manage the young person's involvement with the digital world.

Teenage development – a work in progress

"At the end of the day you're just glad they've got their health, and they're not staying out all night, or staying away from school. Of course we've got issues with him being untidy at home, and not doing things you ask. Some of it is quite wearing. But my son is 15 now, and he is calming down. He's not the most communicative, and he can make us pretty angry at times, but you're bound to have these highs and lows. But I'm hoping. . . . ., and I'm reassured, after all it's a work in progress, isn't it? Everyone tells me they come out the other side, and you can already see it happening. He's changing so fast. It's a stage, isn't it?"

Father of teenage son

Growing up through the teenage years is a process. During this process the individual will constantly be developing and moving towards maturity. The young person will experience a number of major changes that are quite unlike any that have occurred during childhood.

Some people believe that saying it's a 'stage', as did this father, is insulting to teenagers. If an adult responds to some aspect of teenage behaviour by saying "Oh, it's only a stage you're going through", the young person can clearly feel patronised, as if their experiences are not really important because they are time-limited. Responding to this, the Northumberland Health Authority once published a book about young people's health with the title: *It's not just a phase we're going through.*

This is important. We need to be careful and thoughtful when describing the teenage years as a stage. It is the use of the word 'only' which represents the flashpoint. This implies that the young person's experiences do not have any significance, or that they do not need to be taken seriously. Of course this is not the case. It may be true that for many young people being able to understand that moods and feelings are transient rather than permanent can be reassuring:

"I do get moody, I think everyone does at some point. I remember getting very upset about it, and thinking: 'Is this it?' sort of thing. Am I just going to be like this, day after day, live my life like this? And my Mum talked to me, and she told me, like, that everything was transient, and that every mood that I had was going to go away eventually, and so you could be right down, but, you know, eventually it will go, and you'll be back up. It's a bit like 'I'm growing up!' And it never seemed like such a big thing anymore. But yes, there was a point before I realised that, I just felt like, I'm going to be miserable forever, and my life is always going to be in this system, going to school, or work, or whatever, and it's never going to end."

15 year-old girl

What is important however is to take the strength, the reality and indeed the import of the feelings seriously. We as an adult may feel we know – and may be right – that the first love object of a teenager will be forgotten in a year or month or even a week's time. That does not in any way lessen the violence and significance of the emotions experienced. It isn't 'puppy love'. It's love, and you may never feel that strongly again.

Here are some of the major changes that make the teenage years distinctive:

- In the first place these years are a **transition** from childhood to adulthood, and there are particular things about transitions that make them special.
- Secondly, the beginning of this stage is marked by **puberty**, a remarkable and unique process of physical and emotional maturation.
- Closely associated with puberty are the changes that occur in the **teenage brain**. These have great significance for all aspects of development.
- Interestingly there is **no clearly defined beginning or end** of the stage of adolescence in our society, and that too has an impact on young people and on the adults around them.
- Finally the teenage years are characterised by **particular behaviours** that are different from those seen in other stages of life.

Transition

The transition from child to adult means that the young person is never quite sure where he or she stands. Transitions mean that:

- you are neither one thing nor the other
- you are impatient to get to the next stage
- you are excited by new opportunities
- you are fearful about the unknown future
- you worry about losing the safety of what is familiar
- you are confused by new emotions and new experiences

Every adult who knows teenagers will be familiar with the 'flip-flop' of behaviour that is such a feature of these years. As one parent put it: "You never know where you stand. One moment they're up, the next they're down. One moment they want to sit on your lap, cuddle a toy or pet and be fed hot chocolate and marshmallows. Next they want you to 'Get the hell out of my life – what do you know?' This changeable behaviour is hard to live with, yet there is a good reason for it. In essence inside every teenager there is both *a child* and *an adult*. During the transition both these aspects of the individual will be expressed at different times. If you can recognise this it will help you show a little more patience in the face of the inconsistency.

Let us just say a word about being 'neither one thing nor the other'. This state of uncertainty poses special problems for both the young person and for the adult. Everyone wants to feel comfortable in their role. People want to know where they stand, and what is expected of them. This is true in the family as much as it is in schools and work places. Yet during the process of transition this is not possible. Parents and carers are never quite sure how to treat a teenager during these years of development. They may not know themselves how they want to be treated, and it will change from moment to moment.

It is difficult for the adult to determine quite how much to expect of a young person, and how much freedom to allow. Yet, for the teenager, this is tricky too. What is reasonable to expect from the parent or carer? On the one hand the teenager wants to be treated as a responsible person, but sometimes that can be scary. Being looked after and having things done for you can feel safe and comforting. And it can be the perfect excuse not to do something you know is risky or ill-advised when you can say to your friends "I want to do it but my awful parents would kill me!" When the young person's behaviour is looked at in this light, it is not difficult to understand the swinging of the pendulum. If these situations are to be managed, nothing is more powerful than open communication, and being able to listen to each other. Being 'in transition' is never easy.

Puberty

When most people talk about puberty they think of a girl starting her periods, or a boy whose voice has just broken. These are the outward signs of a major process of change within the body that usually takes place somewhere between the ages of 9 and 14. Puberty is the time of the second biggest change in human development. The only time when there is a larger scale of change in the human body is during the first year of life.

It is important to note that puberty involves a lot more than a girl's periods or changes in a boy's voice. Puberty is not only about sexual maturation, or about external body features such as breast development or the arrival of new body hair. Puberty involves changes in the brain and in the hormone balance in the body. It involves changes in blood composition, in muscle growth, and in the major organs of the body such as the lungs and the heart. Puberty also involves a growth spurt, when the individual grows more rapidly than at any time apart from the first 12 months after birth.

Here are some facts about puberty:

- The beginning of puberty is triggered primarily by the release of sex hormones – testosterone in the case of boys and oestrogen in the case of girls.
- All the different changes associated with puberty will last about two years.

- Puberty starts a year or 18 months earlier in girls than in boys.
- There is wide individual variation in the age of puberty and in the sequence of changes. This is perfectly normal.
- The average age for a girl to start her periods at present in the UK is 11 years, 10 months.
- However, approximately one in five girls will have started their periods while still in primary school.
- Although the physical changes will be the obvious ones that can be seen by the outside world, there are emotional changes going on too that are not so obvious.

We should emphasise that there are wide individual differences in the age at which young people experience puberty. Some can start as early as nine or ten, others may not start till 12 or 13. All this is perfectly normal. However in this sensitive stage no one wants to be 'different'. Being in step, and not standing out from the crowd, is very important for young people. As a result many, and parents too, get worried about the pace of change. Some worry that nothing is happening, some that something *is* happening, while others worry about whether things are normal or not.

Parents and carers should be sure that they are as fully informed as possible about puberty. This will enable them to offer support and reassurance, especially when the young person is fretting over whether their development is typical or not.

There are a few individuals who experience puberty either very early or very late. This can cause great anxiety for the young people who are affected, and of course for the adults as well. There are cases of girls starting puberty at seven or eight, and at the other end of the age range there are those who do not reach puberty till 15 or 16. If you or your child has any worry over these issues you should feel comfortable about talking to your doctor.

It is really important for parents and carers to know that none of these experiences need have lasting effects. What is critical is that adults provide the necessary information and support for the young person. If the school is not aware of the situation then the parent should be sure that teachers are informed, so that they too can offer support as appropriate. We should stress that it is unusual for a boy or girl to be so far outside the normal range of experience.

However it does happen, so it is as well for parents to be informed about this possibility.

Research has shown that boys who mature very early usually do well, as they are stronger, taller and more developed than their peers. This often means that they are good at sport, something that is associated with popularity. On the other hand up to now boys who mature very much later than others are not necessarily particularly popular, and do not do so well at their school work.

As far as girls are concerned, both early and late development can be problematic. Early puberty may lead to early sexual interest and activity, and thus to relationships with older boys. Later development can have much the same impact as in boys, sometimes leading to poorer social relationships and less good school attainment. Of course, with the rise of the geek and the respect paid to young people who can manage the digital world with aplomb, this may in the future change. Being able to shine in a digital arena even though you cannot on the sports field may in time prove to be a route to as much respect and popularity.

To conclude this section we will say a word about the possible psychological effects of puberty on the young person. For parents and carers it is important to recognise that, although the focus will be on the physical changes, there will be a lot of emotional changes going on at the same time. Puberty has an impact on the young person's self-concept, and on their sense of self-worth. Almost everyone worries about whether they are normal or not. There is hardly a teenage boy alive who has not worried about the size of his penis, or a teenage girl who has not worried about the size of her breasts. We know from research that the self-image of girls suffers around puberty, with nearly half of all girls feeling dissatisfied with their bodies.

Even the most confident individual may still feel clumsy and awkward as they adjust to the growth spurt and to new physical sensations. Puberty brings with it such big changes to the body that it is inevitable that there will be a period of adjustment for everyone. There are also some differences between boys and girls here. Because of menstruation it is probably true that girls are better prepared for puberty than boys. As an example, research shows that very few parents talk to their sons about wet dreams.

Puberty can be very straightforward for some, and complicated for others. Some remember it as a time of stress and anxiety, others can hardly recall the changes. What is most important is that adults make sure they understand what is involved, and are therefore able to prepare their daughter or son in the best manner possible.

Brain development

> "I suppose what most annoys me is the way he simply doesn't think at times. He's a really intelligent and in fact thoughtful and caring young man. And then he goes and does something breathtakingly stupid – such as going out with his mates and jumping off a bridge at midnight into a river. And when I say 'Why on earth did you do that? You could have killed yourself!' he just shrugs. It was fun it seems and that's all he thought about."
>
> Andrea, mother of 16-year-old

In recent years there has been a remarkable increase in knowledge of what happens to the brain in adolescence. It has always been known that the brain matures during and after puberty. However the latest advances in scanning technology have opened a window on this, and given us access to much more detailed information. These advances have allowed us to take pictures of the brain without causing distress or pain to the individual.

As a result of the technology we have been able to understand much more clearly the nature of the changes that are occurring in the brain at this time. One of the most important findings has been to discover that there is more change in the brain in early adolescence than at any other time of life apart from early childhood. There are many changes going on, but here we will concentrate on three of the most important.

The first is 'pruning'. This may seem an odd thing to be happening, but in essence the brain produces far more neural connections than is necessary. Pruning takes place to ensure effective connections are created. You can think about it like pruning a tree. Dead or unproductive shoots are taken out, and this stimulates healthy growth. This happens at all ages, but we now know that one of the periods of most active pruning occurs in the teenage years. The result is that a lot of change and rebuilding is taking place at this time.

The second is that, as part of the pruning process, new connections are formed and more complex and sophisticated neural networks created. This enables new skills to develop. A good example of this is that the bridge connecting the two halves of the brain develops rapidly at this time. In childhood this bridge is active, but it grows and becomes more important in the teenage years. The development of the bridge between the two hemispheres allows the brain to use its different capacities in a more organised fashion.

The third is perhaps the most important for parents to know about, because it might explain so much about teenage behaviour. Due to the advent of scanning we now know that there are parts of the brain that show especially rapid change and development at this time. There are two sites in particular that are affected, and these are the prefrontal cortex and the limbic system.

The prefrontal cortex is the site associated with thinking, reasoning and problem-solving. The limbic system is associated with emotion, sensation and arousal. The really important finding is that these two sites do not necessarily develop at the same pace. There are big individual differences, but in some teenagers it appears that the limbic system may mature earlier than the prefrontal cortex.

What this means is that, for some young people, there will be a period when planning and problem-solving will come second to having a good time. This is how 'living in the moment' can be a feature of teenage behaviour until the prefrontal cortex catches up with the limbic system. It may be why some young people take risks without thinking fully about the consequences of their behaviour. The search for sensation and arousal may take precedence over good sense.

It is very important to recognise that there are many positive aspects of the rapid brain development that occurs during the teenage years. New skills are being developed, especially in language and thinking. The school curriculum reflects this, as young people take on tasks in maths and science that demand new types of problem-solving. Language too develops rapidly at this time, with teenagers being able to draw on an increasing vocabulary and a wider range of grammatical forms.

Change in the brain leads to the development of new and important skills, but brain development does not happen overnight. The process takes time. While it is going on the teenager may struggle to manage emotions, to avoid risks and to think about consequences and the future as well as the present. If you're struggling, like Andrea, to understand why a normally bright and even sensible teenager throws caution to the winds an awareness of brain development could help. Key aspects of teenage behaviour can be explained by this gap between the development of the part of the brain that says "Hey – that sounds fun, let's do it" and the part that says "Hold on – let's think this through . . . ".

The beginning and the end of the teenage stage

People often ask how long the teenage stage lasts. Not surprisingly parents are keen to know when adolescence begins and, even more important, when it ends. There are no easy answers to these questions. As far as the beginning of the stage is concerned, puberty is usually considered the most obvious marker. However even this is not clear-cut, as puberty can start as early as age nine or ten or, in rare cases, even earlier. Some young people may start to show signs of physical development even though they are still very child-like in their emotions.

The best answer is that there is no one change or specific moment that marks the beginning of this stage. It will happen gradually, with various features of adolescence becoming apparent at different times. Parents may notice some elements of 'teenage' behaviour appearing before others. Signs of a stroppy attitude, or the wish to make independent decisions, for example, may be early indicators that the young person is beginning to move into a new phase. Girls sometimes show such behaviour earlier than boys. It is not uncommon to hear a parent describe a daughter as "10 going on 16"!

There has been much discussion about whether puberty is starting earlier today than in previous generations. Recent research shows that, over the last 50 years at least, there has not been much change in the age girls start their periods. On the other hand other signs of physical development are showing changes. For example girls are starting breast development earlier, and boys' voices are breaking earlier than was the case in the past. Also both boys and girls are taller and heavier than they were even 20 years ago. One of the most likely reasons for this has to do with changes in nutrition.

As far as the end of this stage is concerned, this is even more difficult to define than it is to identify the beginning of adolescence. There is common agreement that it takes longer today to reach adulthood than it did in previous generations. This is because of the major social changes that have taken place, particularly with respect to education and employment. In comparison with the situation 20 years ago:

- A greater proportion of teenagers are staying on longer in secondary education.
- Fewer teenagers are in full-time employment.
- There are fewer long-term job opportunities for young people.
- The types of jobs have changed, with fewer openings in manufacturing and more opportunities in the service industries.
- More young people continue into higher education, with nearly 50% in the UK going to college or university.
- Housing for young people is very hard to find. As a result most remain at home, or return home after college.
- The age of leaving home has steadily increased over the past 20 years.

These facts have a major impact on the lives of young people and, on the way, they achieve adulthood. Most remain financially dependent on their parents, and many live under the same roof. This can lead to resentment and conflict. Even in the best of circumstances, there needs to be a lot of give and take between the generations for this stage to work well for all the family.

Most important of all, this situation means that it is very difficult for an individual young person to know when she, or he, can be considered grown up. How can this be defined? Even more difficult, what exactly does 'grown up' mean in our world today?

Most young people cannot be fully independent from their parents for many years. Clearly therefore financial independence is not much use for determining when someone has reached the end of this stage. As a result young men and young women turn to other markers, such as having freedom to determine their own leisure activities, friendships, sexual behaviour, or drug and alcohol use.

All this means that it is harder than ever to be sure when this stage comes to an end. This can pose problems for parents, and for young adults too:

- For how long should parents go on giving a helping hand?
- Should parents expect their son or daughter to pay rent?
- When should parents give advice, and when keep silent?
- What happens when the two generations have a major disagreement?
- How does the family manage if the young woman or young man wants to have a partner staying longer or even living at home?

The point at which this stage can be said to come to an end is far from clear. Every individual will experience the process of moving to adulthood in a slightly different way. For parents, it is clearly important to recognise the effect that this has on the young adult. The lack of clarity can lead to uncertainty and confusion. Families will need to work together to tackle the challenges. Open communication between the generations will be necessary if young adults are to move into adulthood without too much stress.

In some cultures there are clear 'rites of passage' – ceremonies that mark what they consider to be the beginning of adulthood. In the Jewish community boys have a Bar Mitz-vah and girls a Bat Mitzvah. In other societies adulthood may be marked by a ritual that could include circumcision or scars or tattoos. Most western societies do not have clear 'rites of passage', which may be why young people seek their own ways of saying "You're no longer the boss of me and I'm grown up!" This can be by taking drugs, having sex, joy-riding. Many American schools have for some time had proms – parties at the end of secondary education for which both genders dress up and celebrate the end of one and the beginning of another era in their lives. These have now crossed the Atlantic and are to be found in an increasing number of UK schools too.

Behaviours associated with the teenage years

What sort of behaviours mark this stage as different from other developmental stages? One mother told us that her teenage daughter became irritated when she coughed, or even cleared her throat – teenagers can get annoyed with their parent just for existing.

Young people give the impression of being very self-centred. Their world is the only world, and they appear to live very much for the moment. It may be that this is related to the developments in the brain that are occurring at this time, a process that takes a number of years to complete. As a result there will be times when behaviour will seem to be immature, and what is known as 'adolescent egocentrism' may be one reflection of this.

The teenager can often seem like an actor in a theatre dressing room. They are trying on different costumes, worrying about how they will look to the audience, but not ready to come out on to the stage. The need for privacy during these years is a reflection of the state of uncertainty and confusion in early adolescence. One of the challenges for parents is balancing giving their teenagers the privacy they need and demand, and monitoring to keep them safe. We'll offer some suggestions for managing that balancing act later.

One last example of behaviour that is symbolic of the teenage years relates to the changeable nature of moods and relationships. We have already touched on the flip-flop of emotions that is so common at this stage. The adolescent flips from wanting to be grown up and in control, and looked after and cosseted. They seem to cycle through a revolving door of kindness and sweetness, and truculence and anger. You are their best friend or favourite parent one day, and their deepest enemy the next. This often seems to be one of the central features of teenage behaviour.

We can only emphasise that all these behaviours have their place. They are not necessarily comfortable for the young person, or of course for you as a parent. These behaviours are not designed to get at you, or to hurt you, or to push you away. They are a way of dealing with the pressures and demands of a maturing process. The best advice we can give is not to take it personally. We'll give some more pointers on what you can do in Chapter 9 on communication and in the final chapter.

It may be helpful to keep repeating to yourself that change does not happen overnight. It can sometimes feel as if no change is happening at all. The teenage years are a very long stage, and much of the change will be slow or invisible. Understanding that this is a process of gradual change will help you understand your teenager.

Something for you to try

Here's an anonymous piece from the internet that goes some way to explaining what is happening when your child becomes a teenager. Does it ring bells or could you write your own?

"I just realized that while children are dogs – loyal and affectionate – teenagers are cats.

It's so easy to be a dog owner. You feed it, train it, boss it around. It puts its head on your knee and gazes at you as if you were a Rembrandt painting. It bounds indoors with enthusiasm when you call it.

Then, around age 13, your adoring puppy turns into a big old cat. When you tell it to come inside, it looks amazed, as if wondering who died and made you emperor.

Instead of dogging your footsteps, it disappears. You won't see it again until it gets hungry . . . then it pauses on its sprint through the kitchen long enough to turn up its nose at whatever you're serving, swishing its tail and giving you an aggrieved look until you break out the tuna again.

When you reach out to ruffle its head in that old affectionate gesture, it twists away from you, then gives you a blank stare as if it is trying to remember where it has seen you before.

You, not realizing your dog is now a cat, think something must be desperately wrong with it. It seems so antisocial, so distant, sort of depressed. It won't go on family outings. Since you're the one who raised it, taught it to fetch, stay and sit on command, you assume you did something wrong. Flooded with guilt and fear, you redouble your efforts to make your pet behave.

Only now you're dealing with a cat, so everything that worked before now has the opposite result. Call it, and it runs away. Tell it to sit, and it jumps on the counter. The more you go toward it, wringing your hands, the more it moves away.

Instead of continuing to act like a dog owner, you must learn to behave like a cat owner. Put a dish of food near the door and let it come to you. But remember that a cat needs your help and affection too. Sit still and it will come, seeking that warm, comforting lap it has not entirely forgotten. Be there to open the door for it.

One day your grown up child will walk into the kitchen, give you a big kiss and say,

'You've been on your feet all day. Let me get those dishes for you.' Then, you'll realize your cat is a dog again."

8

Positive parenting

In the previous two chapters we have considered child and adolescent development. Understanding how they develop, what your children need from you and why they may do (or not do!) certain things can help you as a parent. It is now time to turn to the role of parents. Parents will want to know what to expect at different stages of development. Every mother wants to know when her baby will first smile, walk, talk, play with others and so on. However another question that parents will have at the back of their minds has to do with their own influence. Most readers will know the famous Jesuit saying: "Give me a child till the age of seven and I will show you a man". Is this true? How influential are those who play the biggest role in looking after their children?

Over the centuries there have been many theories about the role of parents. Here are four different ideas on this subject.

The 'clay moulding' model. Here the child is seen as a passive lump of clay. The boy or girl is imagined as an individual who can be moulded by the parents according to their wishes. In this model the child is passive, without influence. The role of the parents is pre-eminent. The child will grow up largely determined by the behaviour and attitudes of the parents. This is the Jesuit model.

The 'laissez-faire' model. According to this view, there is little the parents need to do apart from providing for the basic needs of the child. Here the parents are seen as having limited influence. The child will develop as a result of the characteristics he or she is born with. Because of this, the role of the parents will be a small one. There is little they can do to change the way the child turns out.

The 'conflict' model. In this model the needs of the child and the parent are at odds. The child will have wishes and desires that clash with those of the parents. The child is seen as basically selfish. The child expects to have his or her wishes gratified, whether that suits the parents or not. Development is seen as a series of conflicts, the wishes of child and parent being in opposition to each other. In this model the parents are expected to teach the child to give up selfish desires and accept the rules of society. In essence this is the model supported by Freud and other psychoanalysts.

The 'mutuality' model. This model is the one now accepted by most specialists in child development. According to this model both parent and child play a role. The two interact, with both having an impact on each other. From the earliest moments the infant is shaping the parent's behaviour by responding to some cues and not to others. However the baby too is being influenced by the parent's behaviour. Both mother and baby will vary in their responsiveness to each other, thus forming the basic building blocks of later relationships. In this model the role of parents is to recognise the individual characteristics of the child, without giving up on their own wishes and desires. Mutual adaptation, or being responsive to each other, is the best way forward.

Why are these ideas important? All parents will have a model in their heads about what influence they can have, and what role they should play. The descriptions given above may be extreme versions of such models. However all of us will have beliefs about this fundamental element of parenting. Interestingly these models will certainly change as the child grows up. Thus in adolescence some parents may move from mutuality to the conflict model. Others may feel defeated by teenage behaviour, and thus become more laissez-faire.

Parenting beliefs

"I don't really relate to Sam at all. He's another man's child, he's 8, he's already his own person. I concentrate on my own son because I can mould him, I can be important to him. I know it sounds a bit cold but there's nothing there for me."

Daniel, stepfather of an 8-year-old
and father of a 6-month-old

This moves us on to some other important questions about the beliefs that parents hold about children and their development.

- If parents have different beliefs, where do these come from?
- What are the links between the parent's belief system and his or her actual parenting behaviour?
- To what extent does parental behaviour actually affect the way the child develops?

First of all it is worth stressing that beliefs about parenting come from many different sources. Adults will be affected by the way they were parented themselves, although some may say they want to be sure to do the opposite of what their own parents did to them!

Adults will also be affected by the culture in which they live, as well as the values of the historical period. At the beginning of the 20th century it was not unusual for parents to say that "Children should be seen and not heard". Over the course of the last century parenting has become far more child-centred. It has come to be accepted that children's voices should be heard. In addition the child's opinion is now more often taken into account in the management of family life.

As far as we know there are quite strong links between the parent's belief system and his or her actual behaviour. However beliefs have to be tailored to the child's needs and responses. A parent may have a view about what is right and proper, but children differ in their personality and temperament. All parents learn that what works with one child may not necessarily work with another. In this way parental beliefs gradually get modified according to experience.

As far as the last question is concerned, it is certainly the case that many aspects of the parents' behaviour will impact on the child. However as we have noted in the 'mutuality' model, each influences the other. Some aspects of the parents' behaviour will have an obvious impact, such as the type of punishment used. The emotional life of the parent will be important too, as will the atmosphere in the home. Conflict between parents is rarely helpful for the child, whilst love and nurturance, and interest in the child's activities, will always pay dividends.

Parenting styles

> "We tend to balance each other – my husband is far more laid back while I can be a tyrant, as my daughter never fails to tell me. But there are times when I get fed up and throw my hands up and say 'Oh, get on with it then – do what you want!' Needless to say, after a few days of that they're back wanting me to put my foot down, if only for them to be able to have something to complain about!"
>
> Penny, 11-year-old son and 15-year-old daughter

This leads us on to the question of parenting styles. In some respects the idea of parenting styles can be linked to the different models of child development we discussed earlier. What sort of parenting style the mother or father chooses will be affected to some extent by their belief system about child development. The notion of parenting styles was first put forward by psychologists in the 1960s, and has been of great interest ever since.

These styles refer to the different ways that parents behave with their children. Some parents put more emphasis on discipline, whilst others are more relaxed and flexible about what is expected of the child. It was first suggested that there are four different parenting styles.

These are:

- authoritarian – strong on rules and discipline
- authoritative – loving, firm but fair
- indulgent – laissez-faire, allowing the child to do things their way
- indifferent – disinterested

It is important to note that most parents combine elements of more than one parenting style. Mothers and fathers may differ too, so that the child may be exposed to different styles from the two parents. Lastly none of us is entirely consistent. We do not always manage to stick to the behaviour we know is most beneficial for the child. It should be recognised that these styles are a rather idealised picture of different approaches to bringing up children.

Having said all this, it is striking that all the research has indicated that there is one style that is likely to lead to the best outcome for children. This is the 'authoritative' style. Here the parent is warm and loving, whilst also firm where necessary. The parent sets clear boundaries, and lets the child know that there are limits to what is acceptable. The child is helped to understand that these limits will, for the most part, be adhered to. The parent who embraces the authoritative style will also promote autonomy and independence, encouraging the child to take responsibility and to learn to do things on their own where appropriate.

Another aspect of authoritative parenting has to do with being clear about expectations. These will be communicated to the child, so that he or she understands what the goals are. Of course these need to be appropriate for the individual child. It is no good expecting a bookish child to be a sports star! However the authoritative parent will be sensitive to the individual characteristics of each child, and will be able to set realistic expectations. This is important, since everyone needs to have goals, and to be able to judge how well they are doing.

Finally the authoritative parent will have a particular approach to praise and punishment. The parent choosing this style will be more likely to use praise rather than punishment if possible. This means concentrating on the achievements of the child rather than focussing on the things that go wrong. Of course there will be a need for punishment, but this will be used in moderation. When punishment is used, it will be tailored to the behaviour. The reason for the punishment will be explained to the child. The parent will try to be consistent, and will avoid severe or unreasonable sanctions. Research shows that the worst thing for the child is either harsh or erratic punishment. The child should know what to expect if the rules are broken, and should understand why he or she has been punished.

Beliefs about child development, as well as parenting styles, have a direct relevance to the way in which parents manage the digital world. If the parent leans towards the 'authoritarian' parenting style, believing that rules and discipline are important, then he or she will be more likely to want to control the child's use of digital devices. On the other hand the parent who leans towards an 'authoritative' style, believing in the idea of 'mutuality', will want to collaborate with the child in agreeing the boundaries and rules. The 'indulgent' or 'indifferent' parent may not intervene in the child's use of digital devices. This may be either because the parent has no interest in the subject, or because he or she believes these things are best left to the child to work out for themselves. We will return to these ideas later on in the book.

Top tips for parents of young children

- You are a role model. Even from the early years children will be affected by how you behave.
- The brain is especially sensitive during the early years – you can help the process of brain development by close physical contact, talking, nurturance, reading and a recognition of the child's needs.
- However hard it is, try to be consistent in your rules and discipline.
- Praise is more powerful than punishment – three helpings of praise to one of punishment is a good ratio.
- Fairness is important to children; if you have more than one child do ensure that each feels they receive equal attention and goodies.
- Friendships assist development – do help your child make friends and experience social interaction with others.
- Keep conflict between you and your partner to the minimum, or, if that is impossible, keep it out of sight. Children suffer if they witness too much conflict.

The role of parents during the teenage years

Of all the many emotions that parents of teenagers experience, one of the most common is the sense of not having a role anymore. Parents often believe that they no longer matter, since friends and the peer group appear to be that much more important. This is a difficult feeling to manage. If you have the impression that your son's or daughter's friends matter more than you do, you think you are powerless. You feel you are losing control over your own children, and that is a frightening place to be. Even when parents recognise that this has not happened to them, they fear that it will occur soon.

> "One of my fears is that I will not be important any more – that peer relations become more important and there's a transference of talking to, which goes from me to her peers, so she will no longer talk about personal things which she has done up to now. And that I'll lose a feeling of being close to her, in knowing her quite intimately. . . ."
>
> Mother with a teenage daughter

While it is essential to recognise the strength of these feelings, the reality is that parents of teenagers matter. We matter just as much as parents of young children. It is just that we matter in a different way. All the research we have on parenting tells us how important parents are during these years. Where teenagers manage well, it is usually because their parents have been there for them. This does not mean simply giving them money or material goods. It does mean showing an interest and being there to provide support at critical moments.

We can take one good example. Studies of school achievement show that, apart from actual intelligence, the factor that makes the most difference to a teenager's success at school is parental interest and involvement. If the parents are engaged with the teenager's learning, and show that this is important to them, this will provide a powerful incentive for the young person. Of course this does not mean going up to the school all the time and badgering the teachers. But it does mean taking an interest in homework. It means being concerned about how the young person is getting on, and being supportive if things are not going well.

It would be wrong to claim that this works all the time. There are, of course, situations where relationships between parent and teenager are not good. In such a case, the young person may reject the parents' concern and interest. However, broadly speaking, parents do matter. Parents are role models, and they play a key role in many different areas. They will be influential where the young person's health is concerned, they will have an impact on attitudes and values, and they will shape many aspects of behaviour, including the use of online spaces.

Independence

The search for independence creates challenges for adults. It is hard to be told that you are out of date, or that you simply don't understand! It is also hard to learn that your son or daughter prefers to listen to their friends rather than to you. Yet, this is an important process for young people. They need to be able to try out new ideas, and experiment with taking control of their own lives. Unless they have the chance to do this, they cannot grow up and become mature adults.

> "It's so hard when they start questioning your decisions, and what you regard as your wisdom. There are times when it is difficult to be able to cross the barrier between what you think or know is right, and what they want to do. They think you're just being awkward or stubborn, and not moving with the times."
>
> Guido, father of two teenagers

A lot of this has to do with power in the family. Who has control? Who makes the decisions? Since the children were toddlers parents have, by and large, been able to control the situation. Perhaps children have made small decisions, about friends or clothes for example, but in the main parents have held the reins. Mothers and fathers have been able to feel that, when it comes to the important things, their wishes will carry the day.

This situation changes, however, with the arrival of the teenage years. Gradually the power balance in the family shifts, and young people begin to claim power for themselves. They do this in many different ways: through direct disagreement and argument, by becoming more private, or by turning to their friends. It is this shift in power that some parents find hard to manage. And it is this that can lead to the sense that parents don't matter anymore.

Parents do matter

In spite of all this, parents do matter. Someone once said that, for teenagers, the family is like the wallpaper. You only notice it when the paper is peeling away, or when you want to change the colour. In other words most of the time parents are the backdrop, rather than the central feature in the young person's landscape. Nonetheless this should not be confused with the idea that parents do not matter. If parents are not there, or if parents are not providing support, you can be sure the young person will be only too well aware of this.

> "A friend of mine said teenagers are a bit like the terrible twos. They actually need the same amount of time and attention. And I kind of thought: 'What's he talking about?' But I had it in my mind, and I realise it makes sense. We tend to think 'Oh! They're teenagers.' Because their attitude is often a matter of go away, close the door, I want to do my own stuff. But actually if you provide areas of contact they do want that interaction, and they need it as much as in a way the equivalent of what I call the twos and threes".
>
> Terri, mother of 13- and 15-year-old daughters

Parents matter because they provide, among other things:

* warmth, nurturance and love
* stability

- support in times of difficulty
- confirmation that the young person matters
- structure and boundaries
- a role model for everything from health behaviours to managing conflict

Even if it appears that your son or daughter's friends mean more to them, this is only part of a particular stage of development. In this stage it is necessary for the teenager to show independence and to be separate from the parents. In spite of this, there are a myriad hidden ways in which parents will be playing a key role. We will be reviewing examples of how this works in the digital world later in the book.

Authority

In the earlier discussion on parenting styles we noted that there is one style that leads to the best outcomes for both children and teenagers. This is the 'authoritative' style, because the parent is warm and loving, whilst also being firm where necessary. The parent who embraces the 'authoritative' style also promotes autonomy and independence, graded according to the age and maturity of the individual teenager. There are a number of reasons why this parenting style is especially important during the teenage years.

At the heart of the research on parenting styles lie two dimensions of parenting behaviour. These are:

- responsiveness
- demandingness

The parent who would be described as 'authoritative' would be high on both these dimensions. Thus an 'authoritative' parent would be responsive to the individual needs of the young person and, as we have said, would be warm and loving. However this parenting style also involves a high level of demandingness. By this is meant having clear expectations, and communicating these to the teenager. It also means providing firm boundaries so that the young person has a structure that offers a safe framework within which to grow up.

Setting boundaries and limits will lead to conflict. However if this can be done in a way that makes it clear that the parent has the welfare of the young person at heart, rather than the parents' convenience, this will help. It is worth remembering that a clear structure set by parents may not be what the young person appears to want, but without it he or she will be lost.

To summarise then, the most effective way to respond to the teenage years is:

- to be open to the individual needs of the young person
- to show that the teenager is valued and respected
- to set firm boundaries
- to recognise change, and ensure that the rules and boundaries are age-appropriate
- to show that the parent has expectations of how the teenager will behave and what they will achieve

Rules – what are they for?

This is a difficult one, but it links closely with what has already been said. If there are no rules, there is no structure. The young person needs structure to provide a feeling of safety and containment in the home. Of course teenagers will not like rules, as they send a message that the parents are the ones who are in control. Young people will find all sorts of ways to challenge the rules. They may cause aggravation and distress to parents in the process.

However parents must hold firm, and stick to their guns. It is very important that the rules themselves are sensible. Rules for teenagers should have certain characteristics that will make them easier to enforce.

- Rules should be simple to explain, and have a clear rationale.
- Rules should be suitable to the age and stage of the young person.
- If at all possible the rules should be negotiated with the young person, so that they have a say in how these are worked out.

- Rules should be for the benefit of the young person, or for the benefit of the family as a whole.
- Rules should not be set solely for the benefit of the adult.
- Ideally rules should relate to the teenager's safety, welfare or well-being.
- Rules should not be constructed simply because they fit with the parents' beliefs.
- Lastly parents should try and have as few rules as possible. The fewer the rules, the easier it will be to ensure that they are upheld.

What to do if the rules are broken?

The rules will be broken, so that is something that has to be accepted. However if they are sensible rules, then it will be possible for the parent to point out the consequences of breaking them. It should also be possible to show that they are there for the benefit of the young person. Being overly punitive is not helpful. This will only encourage the young person to become more challenging and more distant.

It is equally important that the teenager does learn that there will be consequences when rules are broken. Otherwise what is the point of having them? The teenager may kick up a fuss about any consequences, but the parent should hold firm. Often it is surprising how the young person will, once he or she has calmed down, accept a parent's firm control. This is illustrated nicely in the following example.

"In things that concern their welfare they should have a lot of say, but I do think there are some decisions that parents have to make and stick to them. I found this when my daughter was 16 and wanted to go to parties and things. A lot of her friends did go, and she started stretching me to see how many parties she could go to. One week she had three things organised, and I put my foot down. I said: 'You can't cope with all this and college too.' We had terrible dramas. 'You're ruining my life. You won't let me do anything interesting. I'm a prisoner here.' She was getting really dramatic, so I said she could go to one, but she wouldn't choose. So I said: 'That's it, you go to none.' She didn't go out for a fortnight, and she was quite calm. I think she needed someone strong behind her to be able to do that. There are times you have to be strong and stick to your guns, however hard. Afterwards she did say to me she thought she was being unreasonable!"

Mother of two daughters

Sanctions for teenagers

Sanctions for teenagers will need to be different from those used with younger children. They will need to be age-appropriate, and relevant to the teenager's situation. One parent put it like this: "What is the point of grounding him when we live on a busy road and he hardly ever goes out anyway?" Sanctions used most often by parents of teenagers include grounding (where appropriate), loss of privileges, loss of pocket money, confiscating devices such as laptops, gaming machines and tablets, and setting various restrictions on freedom.

We should stress that there are times when none of these things works.

"I think she's too old to ground now, she's fifteen and a half, and she thinks she's too old. It's almost quite silly to say: 'Look, you're grounded' when she'd be off. It's like: 'Oh, is that all you can do?' She has her own key, she's got her phone, she's got a bus pass. There's no point in grounding her because she'll always go out anyway. You can't keep a kid locked up, and sometimes I think it is better that she is out with her friends, and she does calm down you know! And the funny thing is if we have had an argument, ten minutes later she'll text me, and she's talking as though nothing has happened. It's very strange, it really is very strange! It's just like – back to normal now!"

Terri, mother of 13- and 15-year-old daughters

One of the lessons of this example is that sanctions have to be age-appropriate. Grounding is fine for younger teenagers, but not for those who are 15! It may also be the case that sanctions become less useful or relevant as the teenager becomes older. As this mother says, her daughter already has so much independence that there's not much the mother can do. Once the young person reaches this stage, then rules will be a matter of negotiation rather than imposition.

There are no right or wrong answers here, as each family will have different ideas about what will work with their particular teenager. Once again it is worth noting that harsh or overly punitive sanctions are almost always counter-productive. Finally, if the rationale for the use of a particular sanction can be explained to the teenager, this will make it just that bit more likely that some useful learning can take place.

Types of disobedience

There are many ways that teenagers can be disobedient. These may not always involve direct confrontation, but can include disrespectful behaviour, lying and secrecy, pretence of not having understood the rules, temper tantrums, and obstructive behaviour. Every parent will have their own story of how their daughter or son finds ways of getting round the rules. Everyone will know teenagers who spin stories about the last bus being cancelled, the phone not working, or having to stay late at a party to look after a sick friend. Once again it is worth emphasising that the more sensible the rules, the less likely it will be that the parent has to deal with flagrant disobedience.

It is important to say that there will be some families for whom the suggestions we have outlined here simply do not work. There are young people who do not respond to an approach that involves talking and negotiating. There are some teenagers who treat sanctions as if they are nothing but a nuisance, and do not appear to learn or to engage in sensible discussion. Young people who stay out very late at night, who use drugs, or who get involved with an anti-social peer group will require a different approach.

We cannot pretend that there are any simple answers as to how to deal with these situations. Each is unique in its own way. For the moment we can just say that there will be some teenagers who, for whatever reason, lose that essential connection with their parents that makes the setting of reasonable boundaries possible. While these young people may be in a very small minority, they represent a big challenge to parents and to other adults.

It is very hard for parents to feel that things are out of control. It can lead to feelings of intense anger and frustration, or it can make parents sad and depressed. It is also often the case that this situation creates bad feeling between the two parents, with each blaming the other for the situation.

Many of the things we have discussed in this chapter will help parents avoid a sense of being out of control. Keeping the rules simple, being firm where necessary, taking the young person's needs into account, and keeping channels of communication open will all help to give parents a sense of being in control.

We will tell a brief story to illustrate some of the points that have been made in this chapter. The story concerns the troublesome issue of what to do with mobile phones at night. A mother described how she was worried that her daughter was staying up late at night, talking to her friends on her phone. The daughter was clearly tired in the mornings, and finding it hard to get up for school. The mother decided she would set the rule that, by 10.30 at night, her daughter should turn the phone off and leave it outside the bedroom.

This led to dramatic scenes of fury and resentment. There was much slamming of doors and yelling of abuse. However the mother stood firm, and insisted that she was thinking of her daughter's welfare. On the second night the same thing happened, with more dramatic scenes. The same thing happened on the third night, by which time the mother was feeling anxious about whether she would be able to hold her ground.

On the fourth night the mother was amazed to see her daughter meekly put the phone outside her door and quietly get ready for bed! From that day onwards the question of what to do with the phone at night was never an issue. Many weeks later the daughter confessed that it was a great relief not to have her phone with her at night!

Top Tips

- Stick to your guns. Prepare for the dramas and accusations, but sensible boundaries are essential.
- Concentrate on one issue at a time – and focus on the things that are really important.
- There are many ways to achieve your goal – with teenagers it often pays to wait your time and choose a good moment for a serious discussion.
- You don't always need to win the argument with a teenager – sometimes they need to be accepted as individuals with sensible ideas.
- Encourage adult behaviour – try to help them take on responsibilities and allow room for mature behaviour.
- As one parent put it: "Young people need guidance, they don't need a straight-jacket!"
- Finally, do stay engaged with what your young person is doing. This is especially important where the digital world is concerned.

Something for you to try

Setting some family rules

Every family has rules. The problem is that sometimes we think we all know them and should keep to them but they aren't very clear. It makes a difference if rules are:

- discussed openly
- agreed by all
- sensible and to everyone's benefit

One way of making sure you do this is to have an Ideas Storming session to set them.

Ideas Storming is a technique for finding a solution that works. You start off sitting at a table with paper and pens at hand. You could us a laptop, netbook or tablet but you want each person to feel they are part of this, on an equal footing and focusing on the issue at hand, so everyone needs to see what is being written down. If only one or a few people can see the screen and people are slumped around a sitting room on chairs, sofas or the floor it's easy to get distracted or feel left out.

Warm up – You can warm up for an Ideas Storm, and incidentally see how effective it can be, by asking your group how many uses they can find for a drinking straw, or a button or a DVD disc. Try it – you'd be surprised!

Ask the question – what rules should we have in our family? It is important to be clear about the issue. If you are vague or contradictory you may find it harder to reach a real understand of your feelings or a resolution. It helps to set your mind on being positive and creative – this is not a blame or fault-finding exercise, although it might be important to recognise where responsibility lies. It's about clarifying in order to make the situation better.

The key to successful ideas storming is that initially you put down everything that pops into your mind, no matter how trivial or silly it seems. Don't have rules! Make mum do all the cooking! Everyone should do what they want in their room! Take off shoes at the door. Agree chores and keep to them. Turn off digital devices when we eat together. Eat together at least four times a week . . .

One of you should function as a recorder and a facilitator, welcoming all ideas but holding off discussion of them until later.

Once you have your list, think or talk them over – what was this about, why, when and how? Simply thinking or talking them over can in itself be liberating and lead to insights and decisions. It also makes it clear that you are bypassing the power filter – all of you have responsibility for coming up with an answer and will be listened to.

Draw up a list of rules. Make as many as possible 'Do . . . ' rules rather than 'Don't' rules. Write or print out your list, stick them on your fridge or notice board. Anyone can call anyone out for breaking them, and if they don't seem to be working call another meeting to talk it over.

9

The importance of communication

"I want her to be able to talk to me about everything. I'm convinced that's the only way to keep a daughter safe if they talk to you about everything. It's all about communication otherwise it will all go wrong. Once those communication lines stop I'm sure that's when girls are most in danger."

Sarah, mother of a 15-year-old

From the time the baby first makes eye contact, or smiles, or cries, it could be said that communication is taking place. Communication seems to come naturally, and it is taken for granted by humans as being part of what we do.

But communication is not quite as simple as it often appears. We go from decoding our baby's first cries, to teaching them to talk, to helping them to explain their thoughts and emotions. And just when we think we're on the same wavelength, along come the teenage years when it seems the last thing they want to do is talk to us, their parents. What they are thinking becomes a closed book. But communication is absolutely central to understanding and managing life in the digital age – and we must keep these lines open.

So, why is communication important? Most obviously because communication is the way we keep in touch with our children. How can you know what your son or daughter is doing online unless there is reasonable communication between you? How can you hope to have any influence on them, unless you are in touch?

Conflicts and disagreements will always arise, whether it's about their behaviour around the home, their friends, their schoolwork. In the context of the digital world there are most likely to be disagreements to do with the use of mobile phones, laptops, tablets, gaming consoles, about internet use and online safety and so on. Without good communication these conflicts become much harder to resolve.

Most vitally, it is through communication that we transmit our values to our children. As the online world opens up for them, and new opportunities present themselves, it becomes that much more important that we are able to share with them our principles and beliefs. Open lines of communication are the only way we can hope to retain our influence as parents.

But communication isn't just a one-way street. A child, even a young child, will have an influence on the way communication works. And it always works much better if we pay as much attention to the listener as to the talker. However young your child, the more you listen to them, the more they will listen to you. In this chapter we will explore how to communicate effectively with our children and teenagers.

Everyone is different

"It's odd isn't it? I've got one who never stops chattering. She'll talk all day long if you can bear to listen. She'll even chat to the dog if no-one else is around! The other one, he's not a great talker. You have to squeeze things out of him."

Marie, mother of two teenagers

All of us will be familiar with situations like this. One child wants to talk, another is much more reserved. There are all sorts of reasons why children and young people differ in this respect. In the first place girls do talk more than boys. Girls develop language at an earlier age than boys, and as a general rule girls are more skilled at verbal communication. Of course there are many exceptions to this, but in broad terms language seems to be something that develops more easily in females than in males.

Everyone knows that there are some people who are more sociable than others. We sometimes talk about people as being introverts or extroverts. The extrovert likes other people's company, and likes to share things with others. The introvert prefers his/her own company. Personality differences like this will be reflected in patterns of communication.

Communication will develop in different ways depending on the degree to which children feel that they are being listened to. Here it is important to note that, however much a child wants to talk, the reaction he or she gets from the parent will impact on communication behaviour. Whether a parent is responsive or not will make a difference from the very earliest moments. The baby who first tries to make a sound will learn faster if the parent is paying attention than if they are not.

Age and stage

It is a remarkable journey from the baby's first attempts at saying "Mama" to the skills of a 17-year-old debating the causes of global warming. There are some obvious processes going on, such as the development of vocabulary, the learning of correct grammatical form, and so on. These can be charted and described according to the age of the child. However it should be recognised that development is a slow process. As an example you may be surprised to learn that the vocabulary of a 14- or 15-year-old only contains about 75% of the words in an adult vocabulary.

As a child moves gradually into a wider social world encountering new social situations, so their communication skills develop to assist with new relationships. For example, when the child first meets adults outside the family, such as a nursery nurse or a teacher, he or she develops communication skills to deal with the new relationship. Children quickly learn that just as these people speak to them differently and often with different expectations than their parents, so too must they respond differently. The same can be said of new peer group relationships during the teenage years. Teenagers often use slang and their own language or constructions, both to express solidarity – "Our group shows who we are by knowing and using these words" – and to exclude others – "You don't understand what we're saying" – especially parents. As the sphere of relationships widens so communication skills advance to reflect new social demands.

Within the family communication will develop to reflect the child's increasing independence of thought. As more choices and decisions become available, the child learns new ways to communicate wishes and desires. One of the key elements of communication has to do with disclosure. How much is the child willing to tell, and how much to hold back? When Sarah (see above) says "I want her to be able to talk to me about everything. I'm convinced that's the only way to keep a daughter safe" it's because, in common with many parents, she believes she can only do her job as a good parent if her daughter tells her everything. Of course, this is not going to happen.

Keeping quiet

"He stood in front of us, chocolate smeared all over his 5-year-old face, and totally denied he took the sweets from my coat pocket. He was obviously convinced if he didn't talk, it would be better than admitting what he'd done. It took a lot of persuading that he'd be better off coming clean – so to speak!"

Mandy, mother of 5- and 7-year-old sons

We know that teenagers only disclose certain things to their parents, but even quite young children will be making decisions about what to talk about, and what to keep to themselves. In the early years children know there are some things they should not talk about to adults. Things that are 'rude' and things that might get them into trouble are obvious examples. As children get older, these notions of what to talk about become more developed.

Some important research has been carried out over the past decade or so on what is called 'information management'. This is a term that refers to the way children and young people manage the flow of information from themselves to their parents, something we all do. And this research has enabled us to learn about how children and young people make decisions about what to tell their parents, and how this process changes with age.

The research found that:

- From the age of seven or eight children are thinking about how to manage information; a skill that becomes more developed over time.
- The reasons that children and young people give for making particular decisions about what to tell become more sophisticated with age.
- The older the child, the more able he or she is to take into account other people's points of view.

Children, for instance, may wish to keep home and school separate. What happens between them and their friends can be perceived as private and their own business, so they may tell you some of what is happening but keep back 'secrets' or certain aspects, as a way of feeling in control. Children may also censor their accounts so as not to worry parents, or attract a reprimand. For instance, if they take the long way home to explore rather than keep to the safe route you have agreed.

Research on information management is one of the best examples of why communication is a two-way process, with the child or young person doing as much controlling of the communication process as the parent. We adults all too often have the belief that as it is we who are doing the talking, it is we who are telling the child how things are or should be. But is this true?

In many situations children and young people do not pay attention to everything that is said. Children may only hear half the words that are spoken. If, for instance, you say to a 5- or 6-year-old child "We're going to the supermarket. I don't want you running around shouting as you did last time" the chances are the only things the child will hear are "running around", "shouting" and "last time". Or, "Please don't shove beans up your nose, it's dangerous." Yes – the words that came across, and would probably be acted upon, were "beans", "up" and "nose".

They may show their disinterest through a variety of behaviours – wriggling, looking away, interrupting. Parents may respond by shouting, demanding they listen or even grabbing them. Their actions have as significant an effect on what happens in that communication as do our words. So how can parents ensure in any situation both parent and child hear each other and listen to each other? We'll explore a number of strategies in this book – one of them will be How To Get Your Child To Listen To You and Do As You Ask. This will be found at the end of the chapter.

Active listening

"I think they get what would seem to be negative attention. You're telling them off because, you know, you've told them five times before, but they're still getting that negative attention, and they've got you focussed on them, and it plays on your emotions probably more than on theirs. Because to them you're wrong, you know nothing, you don't understand, and so they're not listening. Whereas I think: why have I not been able to hold the conversation, argue this point, get them to see my way and get an outcome?"

Tony, father of two teenage sons

A key point is that people, and this includes children, are more likely to listen if they think the other person is listening to them. Children and young people often say that parents only want to talk *at* them, but do not listen to their point of view. Talking and listening should go hand in hand. This emphasises the importance of thinking about the listener as much as thinking about the words that are spoken.

For Tony, communication is about trying to get his sons to accept his point of view. He is not thinking about how his communication is being received by the teenage boys. It's easy to get caught up with your own feelings of irritation but the result often is that you cannot get the result you want. This underlines the importance of putting yourself in the position of the listener. What is happening while you are talking? This will help you tailor the message to suit the situation, and increase the chances that your message will be heard.

In Active Listening we make it very clear that we are all ears to what the other person is saying and by doing so encourage them to open up. The key is keeping quiet ourselves while encouraging the other person to feel able to talk to us. We use body language to make it clear our focus and attention is on the other person. We use eye contact, turn towards them, crouch down if necessary to be on the same level. We give full attention, not half an eye and ear while doing something else. We avoid crossing our arms (which gives the impression that we're closed off from them). Then, as the person speaks, we don't interrupt but make the sort of noises – ums and ahs and uh-huhs – and nods that indicate we are listening and want them to go on.

Active Listening can be surprisingly difficult – we keep wanting to interrupt or take over. If we can manage our impatience it can be surprisingly powerful.

Reflective listening

With Reflective Listening we go one step further. The body language is the same and the no interruption rules remain. But now we check out that we've understood by repeating back what they've said to us: "So you're saying . . . am I right in thinking you mean . . .". With young children struggling to use words or string sentences together, we'd wait until they had finished then simply say their words back to them. And we don't laugh or make fun of their attempts and are patient as they make their efforts.

In both active and reflective listening the idea is for parent and child to take turns, each taking the opportunity to be listener or speaker, and to do so for equal time. You listen, they talk then they listen and you talk. It can help both you and your child to have the experience of knowing you will have a certain period of time when you will have the floor and cannot be interrupted, or must listen and cannot interrupt. We'll look more at active and reflective listening and suggest an exercise to try in our final chapter, A Family Digital Strategy.

Block and filters

Whether we realise it or not, we all operate a series of blocks and filters when we communicate. These filters moderate the message that is being communicated. One filter that plays an important part in any conversation can be the power relationship. The simple question "Did you finish that task?" can be heard in entirely different ways when it is one adult asking their partner, a boss asking an employee or a parent asking a child. In the first it can be seen as a benign enquiry. But the other two may be experienced by the employee or the child as the enquirer making the statement "I'm asking to show you I have power over you", and that can lead to resentment and resistance.

Another filter that often operates with young people is that of expectation. If someone expects a message on a certain topic, this is what they will hear, even though it was not intended in that way. A girl who expects her mother to nag her about her untidy bedroom will hear that message, even though the mother may want to talk about something quite different, so a loving invitation to go shopping that started "When you've finished in your bedroom this morning . . . " might result in the child screaming, storming out and slamming the door because she expected this to be a nag about the state of the room and didn't let you finish with " . . . shall we go to the shopping centre?".

There are ways in which blocks and filters can be addressed. For example you can often bypass both expectations and filters by getting into the habit of asking **Open Questions.** A Closed Question is one that can be answered by yes, no or just a grunt. And a Closed Question is usually one in which the parent has already made up their mind about the answer – or to which there is no answer. "What sort of a time is this to come home?" is one of those as is "Do you really expect to go out wearing that?"

Instead with an Open Question we make sure we encourage children to think about what they might say and answer as fully as possible, and also make it clear there is no expectation or agenda around the answer. A Closed Question might be "Did you work hard in school today?" An Open

Question would be "Tell me about your day!" Closed Questions tend to steer children down the avenue of enquiry we've chosen. When you leave it open you might be surprised what they choose to tell you, ask you, share with you.

Everyday chat

"I have found it difficult to communicate with my daughter at times. For me, it's to do with not being listened to, and not listening. Me being caught up in my own world. I get back from work, and I'm tired, I've been giving out all day, and I actually need a break and some time for me, and she may not be sensitive to that. It's the same the other way around – that I'm not sensitive enough to her needs. At that point communication tends to break down."

Hamza, mother of 13-year-old daughter and 11-year-old son

Several studies over the last few years have looked at childhood well-being and happiness in Europe, and in developed countries. One, the Innocenti Research Centre report for UNICEF, looked at a range of indicators. These included healthy living and risky behaviour but it also focused on relationships with family and friends. And as well as asking if children ate their main meal with their parents more than once a week, they asked if children said their parents spent time 'just talking' with them. The UK came bottom in these indicators, and bottom in childhood well-being and happiness.

Making an effort to talk with your children on issues other than the things you'd like them to do – homework, chores, keeping rules – would result in their not always expecting you to be 'on their case'. Asking them for their opinions on screen dramas or the games they play, on how they might solve problems you're struggling with, or inviting them to share what sort of a day they had, all might get them prepared to stop for a few minutes and talk.

Once they can trust that the interaction is not going to deteriorate into a lecture or interrogation they may be more prepared to discuss progress on the homework front, on room tidiness, on fun excursions.

Non-verbal communication

As will already have become clear, communication does not only involve talking. An enormous amount can be communicated through gestures, tone of voice, eye-contact, the way you stand, and so on. This is often called non-verbal communication. All these things convey just as powerful a message as the actual words that are used. You can use very reasonable words, yet by your non-verbal communication you can make it clear that you are very angry. Take the words "I am listening to you". You may want to try and say these words in a number of different ways. You will find that even a slightly different emphasis on a word gives a different meaning to the sentence! It is surprising how much can be conveyed through tone of voice.

Watching what we say isn't enough. How you say it is actually even more significant. Here's an easy way to recognise the importance of how we put our ideas across. Think about the way people tell jokes or funny stories. One person can have you rolling on the floor with a joke or a story. But another person can tell exactly the same anecdote or gag with no effect whatsoever. What's going on? Well, according to quite a few studies, meaning isn't only in what we actually say.

Less than 10% of what we convey comes across in the words alone. Over a third is 'paralinguistic' – that means, the tone or way things are said. You could say "Goodness, that looks colourful!" or "You'll catch your death in that excuse for a dress" or "You look nice!". The words you use may be less significant than the tone of voice, the emphasis in individual words, the degree of negative or positive emotion you employ. A loving parent with a good relationship with a child can provoke an entirely different reaction than a censorious, critical parent with exactly the same words.

Varying degrees of disgust, sarcasm, scorn, dismissal, judgement and anger in your voice transform a simple statement into confrontation – angry words, slammed doors, tears. Yet with a little practice we can monitor how we say things, as well as how our body language sends messages, to make sure our communication with our children becomes a discussion rather than a row.

One important aspect of non-verbal communication, particularly with teenagers, has to do with timing. Most parents know that there are good and bad times to tackle a tricky subject with a teenager. Of course this is true of all communication, but because of the issues we have been discussing, timing is especially important in this context. It makes sense to find a time that best suits the teenager if you want to talk about something important.

We often blurt out a statement, an accusation, a request just as the teenager is about to leave the room, to go out or go to bed. Mostly this is because we've been sitting on it, stewing, for ages and finally lose patience. So when we know we have something to say, it's best to consider what and how we will say it and then choose a time. As all parents will know, teenagers often choose precisely the least convenient time, such as late at night, to open their hearts. Yet seizing the moment can pay large dividends. You may hear things that would never come out at any other time. But often, it's best to say "I'd like to talk – can we get together tomorrow? Let's agree a good time and keep to that!"

How emotion affects communication

"I must say when you do get in an argument with them, and they're saying really nasty stuff, you can say something that to you isn't that bad, but they will take it to heart. In an argument I did once say: 'You remind me of your father right now', and it was the worst thing I could have said. It wasn't until he opened up six months later that I realised what a detrimental effect that one sentence had had. So what I say to people is: be careful what negative things come out of your mouth!"

Bethany, mother of 14-year-old stepson and
8-year-old daughter

So far in this chapter we have been taking a very rational approach to communication. However none of us can be rational all the time. Often emotions get in the way, especially in the relationship between parent and child. It is important to recognise that feelings, such as tiredness, irritation, or frustration, can play a big role in affecting communication.

Many parents talk of getting frustrated. It can sometimes feel as if the child or teenager will not listen, deliberately ignoring what the parent is saying. This frustration is bound to affect how communication works. The more frustrated someone gets, the harder it is to listen carefully, or to take into account the other person's point of view. In these situations 'I' statements can help. There will be more about these in a moment.

It is also the case that in situations where emotions run high, conflict can escalate. Arguments can run and run because of the anger that is behind the words, or things can be said that take a long time to put right again.

It is important to recognise that at times a parent might not want to hear what the young person has to say. In the best of situations parents will want to listen to their son or daughter. Yet sometimes that is very hard to do. As an example, a mother might know very well that her daughter wants her to be at home after school, but the demands of her job could mean that this is impossible. This then becomes an unspoken tension between them. The daughter wants to 'complain' about the situation, whilst the mother does not want to hear. In such circumstances it takes considerable strength on the part of a parent to allow such a discussion.

There is no easy answer to these problems. But, awareness of some of the things we have been saying about communication may help. Emotions, particularly negative emotions, can play a very large role in relationships between parents and young people. Being able to stand back, take a deep breath, and have a break for a few moments is often the best way to manage in these situations. It is also important to remember that the child's feelings of frustration and anger may be more about their own emotional world than about you as a parent.

It's worth becoming aware of your own tone when speaking to your children. If you often sound impatient, annoyed or sarcastic, your children will be less in inclined to listen to you. One mother was rocked back on her heels when she was in the middle of an annoyed rant and her small daughter said rather tartly "Nice voice, Mummy, please . . .". She had to agree her daughter had a point – she took more care with her tone after that. After all, they do what you do, not what you say – if you want certain behaviour you have to model it.

You may need to keep these things in mind:

- Emotions can affect good communication – yours and theirs. Tiredness, frustration and irritation on both sides can get in the way.
- Be aware that if you don't keep emotions under control you may say something you end up regretting.
- You may not want to hear what your young person says – sometimes you have to take on board their complaints if you want them to hear yours.
- It's not always about you! Often, parent and child can be on edge because of elements in other parts of their lives.
- Young people do what you do, not what you say. If you want good behaviour you often have to model it, not just ask for it.

How do we manage when children find it hard?

There are several common issues with children trying to make themselves understood or heard that, if handled properly, needn't lead to conflict or bad behaviour, including:

- Children may know what they want but can't find the words. They'll act up or misbehave to demand your attention but not be able to say why. What should we do? Realise that we can often tell what is needed if we pay attention. Bad behaviour is always about bad feelings so a child acting up, whining or crying, usually has a need that cries out to be fulfilled. Use your knowledge of them and coax them by offering words yourself to uncover the problem.
- Children often interrupt what you're doing or when you're talking to someone else, especially if you're on the phone. What should we do? If it happens again and again you may need to ask yourself if all these other involvements are as necessary as your child, and whether you need to

focus more on them. After all, what's more important? If however you feel the child is being demanding, say "Wait. It's adult time/I have to finish this. I'll be with you in a moment." When you can find a good moment for them, say "Now – what was that?"

- Children often feel they can't wait – to them, it's now or never. And they might fear they'll forget what it was they wanted to say or how to say it if they can't get it out RIGHT NOW. What should we do? You may need to pay attention if they're struggling. If you think they've got to the point where it's a valuable lesson, say "Hold that thought until I'm ready." If it's gone, next time teach them to repeat it to themselves until you can give them attention.

- Children can get into the habit of whining or whinging. It often works – it's like a nail on a shiny surface and we respond to stop it. That, of course, in the long run only results in their using it again since it works. What should we do? Say "Nice voice, please. I can't make out what you're saying if you do it in that voice."

- Children may seem to talk nonstop. Endless questions, endless prattle. It's easy sometimes to want to tune out to get some peace. But this phase doesn't last as long as you think. Once they get to be teenagers, or even as tweens, they might not talk – or at least not to you. What should we do? Make the most of it, with patience and a smile. It's good to be the centre of someone's world.

- Children sometimes don't want to talk. Once they move out into the world and make friends of their own they may want to keep them to themselves. Or they may feel conflicted at the division between playgroup, nursery or school and home, and be trying to keep them apart, to keep them straight in their own mind. What should we do? You may need to use open questions, active and reflective listening to help them feel safe and open up.

The importance of 'I' statements

When you are cross or upset with your child or your teenager it is easy to become critical. You may feel that your daughter or son has behaved badly, or been selfish or careless. In these situations most parents find it hard not to blame the young person. You may find yourself saying: "You drive me mad", "You should have been more careful", "You are just so selfish", "This is all your fault".

People who have long experience in making communication easier have pointed out that placing the blame on the other person is likely to lead to communication breakdown. The other person feels defensive, and stops talking. Or the other person gets even more cross, and the argument escalates.

A different approach is to use 'I' statements. Here you are careful to make statements that are limited to stating your own emotions. You are not accusing or blaming, you are simply stating your own feelings: "I feel upset about what has happened", "This situation makes me feel cross/sad/frustrated etc." You are not talking about the other person, you are talking about yourself. This will allow both you and your daughter or son to be more open with each other.

You will find that using 'I' statements makes it very much easier to keep communication channels open, even if there are strong emotions flying around. If you can own your feelings the other person may be able to do the same, without becoming defensive. It is hard to do at first, but do try. Anyone who has used 'I' statements will vouch for the impact they can have on communication.

When you use an 'I' statement, you are:

- specific about what you want
- given the chance to recognise and say how you feel
- able to help other people understand what you want
- being clear, honest and direct
- able to make your point without blaming, criticising or judging other people

Using an 'I' statement respects the other person and their point of view. It helps you say what you feel and want but avoids making the other person feel like the problem. This makes it far easier for both of you to come up with a solution – they can feel part of the solution, not all of the problem – and to take responsibility and act positively.

It can take some time to get into the habit of using 'I' statements. Most of us have had a lifetime of being told it's selfish or big-headed to say 'I'. But the more you use them, the more you'll find they work and help you and the other person feel good about the exchange.

An 'I' statement:

- describes the behaviour you are finding difficult
- explains the effect it has on you
- tells the other person how you feel about it
- invites them to join you in finding a solution

For example:

> "When I come home and find you haven't done your chores I feel really upset and angry. I feel as if you're taking me for granted and not listening to me. I'd like you to do the chores we've agreed, when we've agreed. If you're having a problem with that, let's talk about it."

Using 'I' statements with teenagers can turn conflict into discussion as above all it respects the other person's point of view and their ability and willingness to negotiate and compromise.

Communication and the teenage years

> "My mum often says to me: 'Why don't you talk about your problems?' I say: 'I do. I just don't talk to you, I talk to my friends.' I have talked to my mum about things, but not at the time they are happening. I tell her about things after they have happened, after I've sorted it out for myself. I still think she wants me to tell her, but I can't."
> 15-year-old girl

Throughout the chapter we have looked at both children and teenagers, but there are some particular things to say about the stage of adolescence. For a variety of reasons communication becomes a special challenge at this time. Teenagers often give the impression that they do not want to talk to their parents, and this can be a most frustrating experience. Parents will say: "How can I get my son or daughter to talk to me?" Why should this be so? What lies behind the grunting, the silences, the arguments?

The first thing to say is that, in this context, communication reflects a change in the balance of power between adult and young person. As the young person becomes more mature, and wishes to express more independence, she or he starts to take a more active role in shaping how communication takes place. This can be seen in many different ways. The teenager:

- only wants to talk at certain times
- does not want to talk at all
- gets cross at being cross-examined
- is more interested in arguing than in listening

This shift in the balance of power is reflected in many different aspects of communication. As a result of the major physical and emotional changes around puberty there is a great deal of upheaval and uncertainty. Because of this there are times when young people feel they need to be in control. They will talk, but in their own time and in their own way. This is partly to do with lack of confidence, but also to do with confusing emotions. Both these factors will mean that it is not easy to talk openly just at the point when a parent wants to have a discussion about something.

In addition it is important to recognise that during these years young people do need a degree of privacy to work things out for themselves. They want to be independent individuals, growing and maturing into adulthood. No-one who is trying to be independent will feel like telling their parents everything that is happening to them.

Managing the digital world – why communication matters

Once you recognise that teenagers in particular are going to want and need to have some control over how and when you communicate, you can see how important it may be to think carefully about how you might keep in touch or indeed monitor what they are doing when it comes to how they use the digital world. Because they want and indeed need to demonstrate their individuality, their separation from you, and their bonds with their own peer group, teenagers will want to be the ones managing their communication with their parents. Digital media and the digital world becomes so important because it is something they feel they own and understand. One of the main messages in this book is that parents need to remain engaged and involved in their children's online activities. But this can pose special challenges, and for many parents it may feel like an impossible task. Engagement with the digital world is such a struggle for parents because:

- **There is a skills gap:** It often appears as if children and young people understand the digital world, whilst many parents do not, or at least understand it less well, or feel less comfortable than their youngsters using it. Young people navigate their way around, seeming to know exactly what to do, whilst many parents look on in awe.
- **It seems to be in a foreign language:** The words used, the page layouts, the images – it can appear to be impenetrable to so many adults. As one example it is hard for a non-player to grasp what is involved in some of the online games. To many parents it can seem as if it is another world that is difficult to access.
- **Young people push the parent away:** Young people will often resist the involvement of parents. This is their own world, where they feel in control and powerful, unlike in the real world. It's something that is theirs, and they may want to keep it that way. This is particularly true in the teenage years, but can occur with children as well. If the child or young person is keen to keep their online activities private, it can be very hard indeed for parents to find a common language and a means of keeping a dialogue going.

All these challenges illustrate why good communication is central to the management of the digital world. Parents can make sure they know something about the technology, and something about the content of games and new websites. To do so, however, depends on cooperation between adult and young person. Parents can keep an eye on what their son or daughter is doing online, but that is difficult without an ongoing conversation in the family.

In the previous chapter on positive parenting, we looked at setting boundaries and making rules. This involves parents taking an active role in monitoring all sorts of aspects of their children's lives, and what is happening in the digital world is no different. Parents need to be aware of what young people can access and how, and set in place agreements about screen time. This should include where their children can see media content, of what sort, for how long and at what times in the day.

In Chapter 11 we will look more at how we can monitor our children's use of the internet, and how we get our young people to accept our monitoring. Communication forms the centrepiece of effective parenting, and in keeping our children and young people safe online. The internet is a playground, with so much that is exciting, entertaining and useful. Like any playground, to be really enjoyable there has to be some risk – too tame and it's boring. But totally unregulated and it's dangerous. By being able to have real conversations with our children and young people – to listen as well as speak, to hear and well as be heard, to be able to lay down rules but to amend them when they make a good case – we can help them stay safe and get the best out of what is offered. That is the aim of this book.

Something for you to try

How to get your child to listen to you and do as you ask

This strategy can be used in all sorts of situations but let's look at the 'going to the supermarket' scenario. You know you're about to go out, you're rushing around getting your shopping list written and your child is playing or watching TV. Usually, a few minutes before or even at the last minute you'd tell them to get ready. You might even try to tell them you're going out soon but you get the wandering attention shtick. So parents can try this. It feels clumsy and artificial and awkward at first. After a few repetitions, and successes, you'll see how useful is this way of doing things.

Twenty minutes to go: go to where your child is, crouch down to their level, touch them on knee or arm and say their name and wait until you establish eye contact. This makes sure you and your child are communicating face-to-face – a great improvement on shouting through a door. It shows respect and a willingness to listen, and means she in turn hears what you say and attends. It also makes the interaction two way – you're making sure she is listening to you but you are also showing a willingness to listen to her. Then say "We're about to go shopping. Want to come and help me write the list? We'll be going in 20 minutes." Then, ask your child to repeat back to you what you've asked – "Are we clear?" You could, if she doesn't repeat it back to you at once, say "What are we doing?" When she does so, thank her.

If she says she wants to go on playing or watching TV or whatever, thank her for answering and say "That's fine. We'll be going in 20 minutes. Will you be ready then?" You may then need to negotiate, to agree delaying a few minutes, or for her to make sure she can record or stream the programme for later, or find a convenient point to pause it. She may, given a direct invitation, be more willing to come into the kitchen and help you or chat with you – in which case, job done.

Fifteen minutes to go: go in, repeat the crouching down, touching, naming and eye contact and say "15 minutes – ok?"

Ten minutes to go: "Ten minutes – you'll be ready, won't you?"

Five minutes to go: "Five minutes – go get your coat." Again, thank her when she does as asked. Keep the contact eye to eye – remember to use the child's name, and a touch on the shoulder, arm or knee to make that connection.

Blast off! If the child has not come running, go in, say their name again, give them a hug and say "Off we go!!". If the child has been grumpy, be sympathetic "It's a chore, but think what we might see on the way! Shall we look for unicorns?" If the child won't come, go ahead on getting ready to go out – don't be drawn in to an argument. By keeping the connection, being upbeat and calm, the chances are even an angry and upset child will join you. Being in charge rather than trailing along behind can make a significant difference – children in supermarkets asked to reach packets off shelves or, if they can read, hold the list and tick off items do not have the time nor the inclination to run around and shout.

Setting them up to making this a joint enterprise does frequently banish sulks and tantrums. And again, always thank the child with descriptive praise when she complies "You helped me with the list, got your coat and came to the door as asked – thank you!"

Key points to remember:

- Be in the same room, next to them.
- Use their name.
- Establish physical contact, and eye contact.
- State what you want, clearly.
- Ask for it to be repeated back to you so you know it's been heard and understood.
- Be prepared to listen and negotiate.
- Repeat at intervals.
- Above all, thank each time you are heeded with descriptive praise.

Making your language appropriate works when children are aged from the time they can understand you, right through primary school. In fact, you can use a form of this with teenagers and even recalcitrant

spouses. "Meal ready in ten minutes – will that programme to be over by then or will you record it?"

As a personal example, Suzie employed How To
Get Your Child To Listen To You and Do As You Ask to
smooth the path of an important family meal:

"It was 20 minutes until Christmas dinner but
instead of telling my 6-year-old granddaughter to
get ready, I asked her to pass the message on to
her grandfather. At 15, 10 and five minutes she
delighted in being the one to go and remind him
they needed to finish their game, then tidy it up,
then go and wash hands together. That it meant she
was prepared and on time was by the by – she'd had
great fun being the one to keep him on track, and to
be in charge."

10

Co-parenting – digital technology when your family is divided

Families come in all shapes and sizes, from one adult and one related child through any combination of adults and children, linked by birth, adoption, fostering or stepfamily, living under the same roof or in different homes. For most of this book so far we've not specified what sort of arrangements we think you might have, although it might be assumed we're talking to families living together. In fact, all of what we have said applies to any family no matter what their form. However, families living apart can have especial challenges when it comes to managing digital use, and new technology can offer both particular benefits, and notable downsides.

What's right for you and what's right for them

"When my divorce came through I just felt like I never, ever wanted to see him again. With two kids that's not, of course, exactly easy. It took me a long time to realise my attitude wasn't helping my children, particularly my son. I thought I was doing what was right for all of us to be limiting the amount of time he was in contact with his father. When I found out he was going behind my back with emails I was furious, until I saw some sense. Let's face it, just because you're divorced that shouldn't mean your kids are."

Bethany, mother of 12-year-old son and 8-year-old daughter

One of the biggest challenges for parents after a break-up is how you work together for the good of your children. It is often difficult to separate what you feel is right for you and what may be right for the kids. Two adults who had a relationship that has broken down often continue to feel hurt, rejected, and a mixture of angry emotions. It can be hard to recognise that in continuing the argument between you to get at your ex-partner, which could feel satisfying, the real victims would be your children. Your motto should be "Love your children more than you hate your ex", and the best strategy is to put your feelings about each other to one side while you both agree to do the best by your children.

When you and your child's other parent live apart access and contact are top issues. You may both see this as being vitally important. Or, you or they may be reluctant, for a variety of reasons. Or, you may feel the other parent's influence so harmful or their behaviour so threatening that you would prefer there to be no contact at all.

It is extremely important for children to keep contact with both parents, whatever might have happened. Children need both parents. Parents have different roles to play. It is usually the father who leaves and because mothers tend to take the main caring role in parenting, it can often be assumed that fathers have less importance. Nothing could be further from the truth. Fathers are important, for all sorts of reasons.

Children and young people often desperately wish to keep contact with both parents, although there can be real issues with divided loyalties. And of course they may feel so angry at the break up that they may initially refuse to see a missing parent. However much a resident parent may see this as a 'vote of confidence in them', they need to resist falling in with it. Children need fathers! Even if this is seldom spoken out loud, children and young people are prone to blame themselves for the separation, and if the connection is broken. They may feel it is they who failed, that the split is their fault. If a parent does not keep in touch the child may assume they are somehow unworthy.

It may be hard to accept but a bad partner can still be a good parent. And what appears to be a bad parent may have dropped the ball because they didn't see a place for themselves in their family when it was together. And now the family is apart, they may either feel they would be doing a kindness to absent themselves, or find it so painful seeing their child that they retreat. Or indeed it can be because the other parent puts so many barriers in the way, they give up. Settling your arguments and putting aside your roles as partners and becoming co-parents is vital.

These are the ways using digital technology can help families where children are living apart from one or both parents.

Contact between parent and child

"Thank you, you were so right to say we should be encouraging them to be in touch more. Since my ex has been making a real effort to text and call every day and my daughter knows it's ok by me to chat with her dad, we haven't had any real meltdowns. Her schoolwork has improved, so has her attitude – her teacher has noticed it. I just hadn't realised how important it was."

Letter to Suzie Hayman, to *Woman* magazine agony page

Laptops, mobile phones and other devices can allow children to choose when to be in touch, giving them a measure of control in a situation they did not wish to happen and in which they otherwise have no power. It can encourage regular minor connections simply to say "Hi, how are you?" or "Good morning!", to build and maintain bonds. It also gets round one of the biggest barriers to maintaining contact in separated families. This is that, as already mentioned, women are mainly the ones to sustain emotional relationships. When parents are apart, children are based with mothers and she is angry with a missing father; she may not make as much effort as is required. Or indeed she may actively block or neglect the child/father link. When children can initiate contact, or contact can go directly between father and child, contact may be better:

"My parents gave my son a mobile phone for his 12th birthday and said it was particularly so he and his dad could be in touch. I was furious at first and said it meant my ex could go behind my back. My mum fixed me with one of those looks and said something to the effect that I wouldn't have even thought of saying that if we lived together and what was the difference? And of course once I calmed down and thought about it, she was right. I have to admit, since he's had the phone they're more in contact and my son has calmed down a lot. We have far fewer blow ups and arguments."

Penny, 12-year-old son

Contact via devices, whether through email, messages or social media, can also be of particular value when children are living apart from both parents. If kids are in 'kinship care', being sheltered by other members of the family because their own parents cannot do so, or if children are in foster care or residential care, contact they can control (with initial assessment and permission, supervision and monitoring) may be of immense value.

Digital technology can also be fundamental in keeping hold of memories important to a child when a family changes. Kids should be encouraged to keep memory boxes, in which they can store cards and letters, photos and items reminding them of family members and happy events. But sometimes these can be lost, or simply fall to pieces after much handling. Uploading photos of people, places, get-togethers, and indeed taking pictures of anything that might be mislaid or worn out, means these stay safe and secure in online storage. Having them online can also mean they can be shared between a child and chosen family members.

"We had such a great night the other night. They came over to stay and I had a box set lined up, but we spent the entire time online going through the stuff we'd all uploaded. Photos, blogs of holidays and weekends and all sorts. They had pix they'd taken of all the shells and stones and other beach rubbish we'd collected on various holidays – they had them labelled with where we found them and when! It was a gas. And we added some more, of us just mucking about."

Fabien, father of twin sons aged 10 and daughter aged 14

Contact between estranged parents

"When I see her I can't trust my voice – I just crack up.
Doing it by email and text, keeping it polite and simple,
makes all the difference."

Father of two teenagers

You may be too angry to want to talk to them face-to-face, too
angry even to trust your voice on the phone – and you both know
if you do have a conversation there is a risk of it descending into
argument. So short but courteous messages via text or messaging on social media can allow you to make arrangements, pass
information, even discuss issues with no danger of conflict. The
minutes or hours in between receiving and returning a message
can allow you to think carefully and be non-confrontational.
Using technology can also make sure you can be up to date on
contact arrangements, fine tuning and rearranging if absolutely
necessary. But never, ever cancelling. This may inconvenience
your ex – it will devastate your children.

Using technology by-passes one of the elements of old-
style separated family issues that children found so hard
and so painful – being asked to carry messages between parents. Do it yourself – there is no longer any excuse not to. If
the aim in using your kids as messengers was to poke, prod
and wound, the people most poked, prodded and wounded
are always the children.

Co-parenting

"We had some little differences when we were together
about things like discipline – I'm a bit easier than he is.
Once we were separated these seemed to get further and
further apart and it's as if he's turned into this Victorian
father and he thinks I'm totally hippy dippy."

Ally, mother of 10- and 13-year-old daughters

Social media can allow separated families to operate as one.
You can tweet with hashtags so you and children join in a
conversation between you all. You can upload comments
and conversations, photographs, videos and memories to
a private website or social media page that all the family

can access and share. If you can no longer chat around a shared meal table you can offer your children the chance to do so within a shared space online. Non-resident parents often miss out on the achievements and creative output of their children. The resident parent may remember to show school books or art work on visits, but these can get lost in the chaos of handover. Uploading all digital output or links to it, and pictures of real world items can mean a parent living under another roof has a chance to see their child's development and production when apart, or when the child is with them and eager to show off.

Knowing what is going on in their children's lives means parents can keep a dialogue going about rules and boundaries and what is important – these change as children grow but if you're not sharing, one partner can be left out of the loop. It means whoever is looking after the child has a chance to share both triumphs and anxieties with the other responsible adult and ask for support. Young people can really benefit from the extra oversight – more adults able to say "I've seen what you did there – it's excellent. Have you thought of trying . . . ?"

Children can cope with different rules applying in different places – school, home, grandparent's homes can all make different demands and expect different behaviour. Parents living apart may also have different styles and these can be managed as long as there is discussion and room for negotiation. What is needed is agreement on the essentials, a respect for what one of you might wish to say is a priority, and an understanding that the people who suffer if you can't agree are the children, not the ex.

Contact between children and other family members

"Why should they get the chance to see him grow up if my own mother can't?"

> Mother whose own mother had recently died on why she resisted contact between her ex's parents and her son (family taking part in TV series *Stepfamilies*, with Suzie Hayman)

Grandparents, aunts and uncles and cousins can often lose touch after a family break-up, especially with the extended family of whichever parent has less access and contact. Commonly that means the paternal grandparents who might have relied on their daughter-in-law to manage arrangements to meet, who now might feel detached from or even hostile to her ex's family. Children love and need grandparents – both sets of grandparents. And often thrive with contact with other family members. Digital technology can help make those links easier.

Contact between both parents and other adults involved with their children

"I wasn't in favour at first – I felt it undermined them sending stuff to him because I was the one looking after them, day to day. Then I overheard him talking to our eldest about a school trip and I realised he was supporting what I'd said, and our son felt really good about it."

Mother of 11-year-old son and 9-year-old daughter

Non-resident parents are more likely to feel detached and frozen out if they experience little of the day-to-day contact between parents, their children and establishments such as school, dentist, doctor, social workers. Most of these now recognise the need to keep both parents involved after a separation. Unless there is good reason for the contrary they should duplicate contact, using texts, messages or access to online information, so that both parents know what is happening in their children's lives. And when children are on a contact visit, they do not miss appointments, forget to do homework or turn up lacking essential equipment or clothing.

Contact between children and supportive friends

"My son's school had a project going with email contact with children from a school in America. I heard an awful lot about this boy he was chatting to but it wasn't until the teacher remarked on how much it had helped my son that I found out they'd been drawn together because both were missing their dads. My son got an A* on a piece of work he did on the differences and similarities between separated families in the US and UK. Far more important, he and this boy clearly really helped each other through it."

Bella, mother of 15-year-old son

We hear a lot about cyberbullying and trolling – about the internet and social media being used in destructive and decidedly unfriendly ways. We hear less about the fact that many young people find support and consolation from friends online – both from people they know in the real world and people they meet online. Being able to post on social media about anxiety, confusion even anger about family change can allow a young person to hear from people who are in or have gone through similar situations, who can offer sympathy and suggestions.

How can digital technology be a problem in separated families?

Many of the advantages and the drawbacks of digital technology are the same whatever your shape of family. But there are some problematical issues that are particularly likely to occur in a family that has undergone change.

Relaxing rules

"All my friends thought it was marvellous for him to buy them top of the range tablets for Christmas. They don't see the other side of it. It's bad enough he lets them stay up late when they're with him and it's always 'Why can't we do this, dad lets us . . .'. But now it's 'I want that, why don't you buy it for me, dad would . . .'. I know it's just guilt that makes him do it, and it would be fine except it's making life hard, not just for me but for them too."

Tanya, mother of 9- and 11-year-old daughters

Parents may find themselves being more lenient about all sorts of issues after a break up. It's not uncommon for both parents with main responsibility and parents with access to lighten rules, relax boundaries and let children off chores or homework in the process and aftermath of a break up. The thought behind this is that since they are having such a hard time, letting up may help. Parents may want to offer their children what they see as special consolations and treats to make up for what they are undergoing and losing, and digital devices and free access to them can seem an ideal solution. As we've said, children can cope with different rules in different places. What they can't cope with is if one parent is either being inconsistent or using rule changes to attack or score against the other parent. If this is happening, parents need to communicate to settle their own issues with each other and not let their disagreements harm their children.

And indeed, digital technology may become an essential tool in keeping contact and a connection between child and non-resident parent, and in being able to find support from other family and friends. But failing to set boundaries in such circumstances instead of being a solution or a comfort lays children open to risk. Observing rules and boundaries, and even doing chores or being expected to maintain efforts at school or home, far from being onerous, give structure and security. You may find children in such circumstances pushing back at you when you do assert control or reinforce rules. However hard it may feel, it's still so important to hold the line.

One foster parent told us:

"We were asked to go to her school and were told our foster daughter had been cyberbullying another girl. I had to confess we really hadn't understood what she does on her phone and were afraid to ask. We got it sorted and in fact, it helped our relationship – she could see we were there for her, even when we didn't like what she'd done. But it did teach us to keep closer checks on what she was doing online."

Children left unmonitored can stray into all sorts of undesirable sites and consequent behaviour online and off.

Unhappy children left to their own devices may not only seek out inappropriate and harmful areas, they may find themselves targeted by dangerous outside influences. And of course they may 'pass the parcel' of their own unhappiness by making life miserable for someone else. In all cases, they may feel unable to come for help or support. This could be not only for the usual reasons of thinking they may get told off, but because they think you have too much on your plate for them to bother you.

Dangers of contact

"I can't let him anywhere near the internet. He thinks his father has gone off and abandoned us and that's better than telling the truth, that his father's been done for violence against me and his family have threatened worse. We've moved but I live in fear of them tracking me down so I can't let my son put anything up that could let them find us."

Mother of 7-year-old son

These are not common experiences but they are so important for those who are affected, we need to highlight them. Taking your eye off the ball when you have other things on your mind can, as we've shown in Chapter 2, expose your children to all sorts of risks. But when families have undergone change there may be additional dangers. Contact with both parents and with other members of their family is vital to children. Indeed, the courts now recognise this and have abolished the concept of custody, which was about adults owning their child. Now we talk of residency, access and contact, which enshrines the child's right to have contact with their family. Even when there has been abuse between adults, or indeed, from adult to child, the child will still want and need to have some contact, to feel whole and worthy. In such cases Child Contact Centres may be the answer, where parent and child can see each other but under professional supervision to make sure all is well. But if concern has been shown to be present there may be situations where the parent caring for the child should take particular care over online use, both for themselves and for the child.

You may have to be especially vigilant about your child's online use – not only under your roof but with friends, other family members and at school or during out of school activities. If you have a reason to need your child's whereabouts to be kept from anyone, be aware that any pictures or text about them in the public domain could be searchable. If you or they want to put anything online where friends and some family can see them, you need to use privacy settings and be careful about who can see your content. You also need to ask all your contacts who have access not to share or copy anything, if that takes the material out of your secure area into a more accessible place. And to impress on your children not to have an online presence that could be found. This might mean their being unable to be on some social media pages – the sort of pages their friends have and share. This may also mean asking teachers, youth workers, other professionals, to be alert when anyone is taking pictures to make sure your child cannot be identified.

This may not be easy. Other adults may find it hard to accept why it could be important and your children's friends may either not get it, or forget how important it could be. Having to step away when group pictures are taken, or ask friends to remove pictures or remarks that could be used to trace a child can be painful for children. As one parent said:

> "My son's father is the subject of court proceedings and it's so important neither he nor his family know where we are. My son was gutted that this means he has to be anonymous on social media and can't have pictures posted. He hates it and found it really hard to explain to his friends. Then one mother, who fosters and also has to keep her child under wraps, came to our rescue. She got all their friends to think of it like a spy having to keep cover. It's now a game but one they all take really seriously."

It is surprisingly easy to trace people through the internet. Whole websites have been set up and some have been running for years based on searching for friends or family members. Often the reunions are happy and fortunate, with all parties benefitting. Sometimes, they are disappointing and do not come up to expectations. And sometimes, the result is problematic. Digitally savvy young people often do not need help to make a search, and determined adults can learn how too, or take advice. Finding information is especially easy given the fact that many social networks automatically show locations when users post. And any digital photograph uploaded has 'meta-data' attached with gives enough information for the place and time the image was taken to be found. You can also do an image search using printed photos to find the place shown. A young person could, for instance, use pictures in their life story books or boxes to find the real-world location of an old home or neighbourhood where they had been pictured with a family member with whom they are no longer in touch.

Contact arrangements

Digital technology can revolutionise contact arrangements. There are several issues here. One is that it is vital for children to stay in touch and have regular and, most importantly, predictable contact. They need the security of knowing the non-resident parent will stay in their lives, and they will see each other at such and such a time. There is however a difference between what young children and teenagers need and want. Children do require the parent themselves to make these arrangements and for both to stick to the arrangements. Neither should let the child down by cancelling. Teenagers on the other hand need to know the non-resident parent is there when they need them and is present in their life. But because their own social life is so important, they need to have flexibility and be able to play a part in making such arrangements themselves. In both cases, online scheduling tools such as Doodle give everyone the opportunity to find mutually beneficial times to meet and to arrange them. This can be done in their own time and doesn't necessitate phone conversations that can sometimes become acrimonious.

Dealing with family change and vulnerable children

Digital technology can breach boundaries. Before such access, a parent or a professional responsible for a child's wellbeing could be certain that when they wanted a connection broken between a child and previous family members or other contacts, it would in all probability stay broken. Sometimes this is for good reasons. Continuing contact could be harmful for the child. It might undermine a child's ability to feel safe and secure and at home in a new situation, when for instance someone is actively telling them to defy or ignore the requests of the adults with whom they are living. Or an adult may be making false promises or unrealistic plans or continuing emotional abuse. With all the possibilities of the internet, such boundaries can be blown apart. Bringing young people and lost family members together is not always a desirable situation or not at least without considering the consequences and putting checks and support in place.

Gaming in family change

> "I was grumbling to a teacher about the amount of time my daughter was spending playing online games with her dad and he said 'Oh, is that why she's suddenly getting As for her history projects?' I hadn't thought – what they're doing is all beyond me. But when I asked, it was true – they're doing some sort of treasure hunt but it's all in Tudor times and that's what she was studying. So I started to see it wasn't just that the two of them were spending time together she enjoyed, she was learning something. And he was supporting her in school, too. All good!"
>
> Lynne, mother of 12-year-old daughter

We've put gaming in families in the process of change in a section of its own because it is such a large and complex subject, which can have particular value when families are having problems. There are, however, both good and bad aspects.

The bad news

Let's get the bad aspects out of the way first! Gaming can become a retreat for young people if their family is in conflict. If real life has become stressful, painful and confusing the safe boundaries of a game, with its easily understood rules and consequences, can be a welcome retreat. Young people can assume a different persona, of someone competent and capable and in charge, as a way of stepping away from the feelings of guilt, hurt and anger they may be experiencing. From a retreat it can become an addiction if they can't be helped to recognise whatever is going on isn't their fault, and that they can learn other coping mechanisms.

Some of the lessons they may take from some games can also be less than helpful. Such as, that violence is the answer. Or that you should expect immediate solutions, and that other people can be manipulated to do what you want. Or indeed that some of the things you view in some games and on some internet sites, such as misogynistic attitudes to women and sexual violence, are normal.

Now for the good

But gaming can be helpful in many other ways. Gaming can teach young people patience and persistence – to try again to find a solution if one doesn't emerge at once. They often learn that big changes come in stages and can only be affected if you do it little by little. Two-person or multiple person gaming helps young people to work in collaboration – to realise you have to communicate with those around you. You need to discuss, explain and share ideas and responsibilities to succeed in many games, as you do in real life. Gaming can give young people a community – a sense of belonging, and people to talk to. This may restore or build self-esteem and confidence at a time when they might have lost them. And it may teach them that sometimes you have to accept failure, and that what other people do can take the game out of your hands. You're not, in other words, always responsible.

Children and young people living apart from family members can find in games a shared space in which they can meet. Children can find it hard to communicate – chatting on the phone or even through text can be stilted and difficult. But they may be more than happy to share game time, and while doing so feel connected even when geographically apart. Using games such as *Minecraft*, children, young people and family members can build a place of their own where they can feel they belong and can meet. When they do meet face-to-face again, using the game can bridge awkward 'getting to know you again' moments.

The benefits of digital media in family change

So, what are the benefits of using digital technology and social media?

- **Ongoing, cost-effective contact, in the control of the child**: Where contact is helpful for and wanted by the child, digital media allows many different ways of communicating and keeping in touch, from Skype and FaceTime to regular check-ins on social media. This can help children who are now some distance from family members, or where either party may be unable to visit as often as liked due to family or work commitments, illness, cost, disability.
- **New ways of communicating**: digital media, including texting and social media, offer children and young people ways of communicating other than through face-to-face speech, which many find intimidating with an adult. Young people often find it easier to be in contact via text or to express their feelings and ask questions through a video. It can also help young people find places and people that can help them, via websites designed for them.
- **Keeping hold of memories**: many sites help children and young people keep hold of important places and people in their lives, via pictures and videos, text and other media, in safe online storage. This can be shared appropriately or simply maintained. If children and young people live or periodically stay in various locations they can still have items at their fingertips to show those they are with.

- **Feeling 'normal'**: taking part in activities such as gaming can help children and young people, including those with disabilities, feel respected by and attached to others, especially if what is happening or has happened in their family makes them feel singled out or disconnected.
- **Family-finding**: when a child or young person's immediate family has separated it might be important to them to be in contact with members of their extended family – grandparents, uncles and aunts, cousins. If contact with them has lapsed, the internet can be used to find them and renew contact, face-to-face or through social media.
- **Finding a voice and community**: social media enables young people to talk to each other, share experiences, and support each other. This can be especially valuable when they might be experiencing difficult issues. It means they can continue to be able to talk with and get help from friends out of school – evenings, weekends, school holidays. And it can offer the chance of talking with people in the same situation, who live elsewhere. Not only can this offer more possibilities of mutual support but it can help young people see they aren't alone in their experience or their feelings.

Something for you to try

This can apply to all families, but has especial relevance and use to families that have undergone change. Help your child/children/young people put together a memory box online. This can include photographs, both digital and prints that you can digitally convert; videos; links to apps with content they would like to keep track of; photos of items they own, records of birthdays, holidays and other important information and anything else to do with their family and family experiences, past and present. Make a date to spend time looking through these regularly.

11

A family digital strategy

We've looked at the worries many parents have about the digital world. We've explored whether those worries have substance. There are indeed concerns and even threats our children can encounter when using digital technology. But there are also fantastic opportunities. Armed with a greater understanding of how your children develop, which gives you clues as to what they need from you as well as why they may be so drawn to the allure of digital technology, we'll now turn to what parents can do when faced with the challenges of the digital world.

You assume as a parent that your job will be to bring up your children. That can mean helping them to develop and become the best they can be, to become social beings able to get on with others, and to learn boundaries and keep themselves safe. We don't let them out alone until we feel they know road safety, and we watch and guide as they learn the ropes. In some cases we struggle to lay down and be firm about rules – children and young people may resist, and we may not feel confident enough to insist. Screen use seems to be one of those issues that many parents find difficult. And in so many families we seem to have lost the plot when it comes to mobile phone, gaming console and other device use. We don't monitor, we don't set boundaries, we haven't created rules.

In our research for this book we realised that digital technology, social media and the internet are not quite the dangerous and terrible things some studies and much of the media seem to be saying they are. The warning we would like to sound is not about the thing itself, but how you use it. There are dangers but there are also wonders out there – used with care and attention, the digital world can be a revelation. What is clear is that parents need:

- some knowledge
- some understanding
- some skills

to manage this important new aspect of home and external life. You can't, and really shouldn't, fight it. Best to subvert it to your own ends!

So the skills we would like to encourage you to develop and use are not about putting the lid on digital use. The key is to know what your children, whether primary school age or teenagers, are encountering and to help them manage it safely and positively.

How it affects you

Parents may feel incompetent and incapable in the face of a technology we might think is beyond us, or that the genie is well and truly out of the bottle. Or, you may have accepted quite a few aspects – using social media and accessing enhanced opportunities of entertainment via streaming services yourself. The digital revolution has also meant more of us bring our work home, either by actually having flexible working where we spend some or most of our time working in places other than an office, or by bringing work or accessibility home with us. More and more employers are taking advantage of technology to contact employees at any time – day, night or weekend – and feel they and their employees ought to be 'always on' or, if not, they will be showing lack of commitment.

How you behave and what you believe has a profound effect on your children. You are a role model and they will do as you do, not as you say. If you are anxious about digital technology it won't stop them using it but it may mean they hesitate to bring you any worries. And most important of all it may mean you set no rules or boundaries, or inappropriate ones. Bad rules tend to be ignored or flouted or lead to needless conflict. If you are a confident user however, you may be passing on other messages, not all of them helpful.

We need to understand the positives and the negatives of digital technology and its use. We need to negotiate rules and sanctions and keep an eye on how our kids are managing. Before we do any of that, we need to understand how digital technology, and our own and our children's use of it, often makes us feel.

In a word, that can be anxious. However 'tech savvy' you may be, however much you may use mobile phones and computers and access social media and the internet, the chances are your children, whether of primary school age or teenagers, will be more proficient. Or will be very soon. When you don't understand something it can feel as if you are losing control. You don't know what they're up to, and your anxieties can mean you exaggerate the threats, and don't recognise the benefits. Telling kids the sky will fall if they do certain things means that when they do it, behind your back, and the sky doesn't fall, they conclude you know nothing and can be safely ignored. Or, that if something awful does happen they can't come to you for help because you'll say "I told you so!"

What can you do?

The first strategy is to address your own digital use. It's already been said, but let's repeat it. Your children do as you do, not as you say. We cannot overemphasis the importance of the parent as a role model. Even as teenagers, when friends become an important focus, they will still listen to you and watch what you do. And of course, by the time they become teenagers they've already had 13 years of following your lead.

We are going to have to monitor and mediate our children's use. The eventual aim of course is for them understand the reason for your boundaries and rules and so in time be able to regulate themselves. Until they can, you provide the structure and the encouragement to be safe. If we're going to set and ask them to keep rules and boundaries we have to be consistent and keep those rules ourselves. If when you're home you spend time checking social media, if a television is always on, if digital technology is always to hand, that's what they will know is normal behaviour. If you're always available to people outside the home they will note that.

If adults are constantly available to their employers they will soon get burned out, losing rest and relaxation time. Families suffer as time together is eaten into by work. Even if it's for social reasons, young people get two destructive messages – one, that constant online presence is not only desirable but mandatory. And two, that they are less important to their parents than people outside the home. Parents need to make it clear to their employers that contact is restricted to the hours contracted and phones will go off at other times. Since beginning to write this book one of the writers has established the habit of switching off the computer and mobile phone for the night sometime between 17.00 and 18.00. The sky has not fallen.

If we are to address their anxieties about FOMO – Fear Of Missing Out – we have to address our own first. The world will still be there when we switch on again the next day. It helps if we return to having separate devices for many of our social needs rather than putting it all on the phone or tablet. If your main device wakes you up, plays you music, takes your photos, lights your way, you are pressed to have it with you and on at all times. Which means those tones will be calling you to take a text, join in the conversation, be wired in. Buy an alarm clock, a camera, a music player, and a torch, and switch off the phone and tablet.

We need to gain some technical know-how to exercise control. Ask the shop from which you buy a device exactly what it does, and what you can do to make it safe. Don't, for instance as some parents did over Christmas 2013, give small children tablets loaded with apps that not only allowed them to play at the sort of fun games young children like, but through those games to say yes, repeatedly, to online offers of add-ons – add-ons that ran up bills amounting to hundreds and in some case thousands of pounds before parents were alerted. Ask your friends what issues they have had and what advice they can offer. And, above all, ask your children what they are doing and for them to show you.

Sites such as Internet Matters (see appendix) can give valuable advice and support on many aspects of keeping your children and you safe online. And all social media sites offer FAQ (frequently asked questions) pages which can show you how to locate and permit privacy settings and other vital safety measures. Privacy settings enable you to dictate whether anything you post is to be seen by only your friends, friends and friends of friends, or the whole world. Use them!

How it affects your family life

When we talked with parents many of them agreed on the issues that worried them. One was that digital technology was a distraction, that it came between them and their children and takes up too much time at home. They felt hurt that their kids seemed to pay more attention to friends than them, and this often led to family conflict. To manage digital technology, first you may need to look at your family life and your relationships with your partner and kids. If you've got those aspects of your life sorted you'll be able to transfer the skills that keep those running happily and smoothly to managing digital technology. If you're experiencing problems, the first thing you need to do is address those issues. We'll signpost some places to go for further advice and help in the appendix.

Be prepared to ask for help for you or your child or your family as a whole if you have any level of problem. Children do not get addicted to digital technology simply by being in contact with it. Destructive behaviour arises when there is the perfect storm of access, and a need for some sort of escape, affirmation or support. If you and your partner, or you and your children, or your children individually are experiencing any sort of emotional difficulty get help – your own GP can offer counselling and mediation or use one of the many tried and tested organisations we recommend in the appendix. Digital technology becomes a problem when you aren't using other ways of resolving conflict and unhappiness.

Another common issue mentioned by parents was when to begin thinking about setting rules around use. Most felt that it wouldn't be an issue until their children were in their teens. But is this true?

What can you do?

You and your children need to be talking. If you chat with your children about trivial, everyday things, and listen as much as you talk, two things happen. One is that family happiness increases. The other is that they will come to you when they have something important to ask or say.

It's obviously easier if your family is young and you can set these rules now. Even if you have teenagers you can still go back and reset. It just takes some persistence because you may at first get resistance. Persevere – it's worth it.

Rule 1

Focus your attention on your family.

Start off each time you get together after a day at work or school on the right foot. You want to remove any barriers to listening and talking with the people with whom you share a home. If you begin with conflict or by ignoring each other, it's hard to mend the situation later on.

> "Every single evening was an argument. I'd come home and my daughter would be on my case, my wife would want me to deal with the kids, my son would be in his room and before you know it we'd be shouting. So I did what you suggested. I had ten minutes of my own before joining the family – I had a shower, changed and listened to two tracks on my headphones. Then, I was theirs. Just that period of separation from work and home and that time for myself calmed me down. Do you know, the arguments stopped and only because I wasn't in an instant bad mood. Having had some time to myself I could give my attention to them."
>
> Simon, father of 13-year-old daughter and
> 10-year-old son

As Simon found, when you're stressed, especially when you're trying to make the transition between work or school life and being with your family, you can feel upset and soon lose your temper. Because you all still have half your attention on what has been happening outside you can't give each other full attention. Having a few minutes to calm down and put outside matters to rest, you can all give each other the attention you deserve and need.

Rule 2

Switch off for the first half hour

Of course you may quite rightly feel that totally cutting off all external connection for the evening would be a step too far – your children will definitely think so. But making a point of beginning the time you spend with family as being a period when you concentrate on each other can set a helpful tone. How do you do it? Matter of factly. Turn your own phone off and invite your children to do the same. Give an inducement for everyone to comply – serve drinks and biscuits round the kitchen table and chat. Use open questions. How was your day? Tell me about what you did you were pleased with? What did you wish you did better, and how will you do so tomorrow? What did you see or hear you'd love to tell us about? What's the new film/box set/reality programme everyone is talking about – what do you think?

Model the ability to let go of your phone by parking it somewhere – near the front door, on a kitchen shelf – and invite them to do so too for that all important first half hour. Put your phone and device chargers in this area too. Everyone's phones and tablets stay in this place overnight, not in bedrooms.

Rule 3

Eat as a family round a table as often as possible. And ensure that there are no phones or other devices for anyone at the table.

This is a hard one for families when so many of us have evening activities – both you and your children may have calls on your time that make it apparently impossible to find any time when you're all together. You need to look carefully at all those activities and prioritise. A minimum of three evenings a week together round a table would be so valuable that it would be worth letting some of them go. That's a minimum – we would like to say it should be every night even if it means adjusting the time you eat and the things you do to make sure everyone is there.

Some families say the main difficulties in getting kids round a table might be that they don't all want to eat the same food, they will refuse food they don't like, they won't let go of their devices, they don't want to miss something on television.

The obvious answer is never, ever let your children get to this stage! Food you put on the table is the food you all eat, together. Yes of course you respect individual likes and dislikes but often these are more about asserting some sort of control over their lives than real likes and dislikes. If you've let your children pick and choose their food it is hard to wean them off this idea. But it is possible. One tactic is to get them involved in cooking and preparing the food in order to engage them and help them understand the whole dinner-time process. Cooking food from scratch is actually not that much slower or more difficult that using pre-prepared and has so many advantages. It's healthier, cheaper and, most of all, allows you the opportunity to chat and bond, and cook something that everyone will eat. When they cook the food they tend not to turn their noses up at it.

Then, don't serve any food until the devices are put away ... and keep this 'no-devices' policy throughout the meal time. As before, offer inducements. Give them a platform; ask them the best and worst things about their day, and then let the conversation move in ways that they really enjoy. Listen, laugh, enjoy their company and what they have to say. Tell them they can check in with social media at a specific time after the meal. See how long you can keep them chatting to you – it may be longer than either of you expect.

As for not missing anything, that's now easy. New technology means that any programme can be time shifted – watched later, on demand. If their argument is that half the fun is being on social media commentating as the programme unfolds, use that as a springboard for a discussion on the importance of their being able to comment in real time on everything with everybody. And ask them to prioritise – is there one programme a week during which they'd like to be able to do this? You can use permission as a reward, or withdraw it as a sanction.

Talking together more also helps you practise the skills of dealing with parent/child and parent-to-parent conflict. Even before you deal with issues around digital technology you need these skills. We've explored some positive parenting techniques in earlier chapters – how to use 'I' messages and active and reflective listening to communicate with your children. And we've touched on sanctions and how to set some family rules. You may find a couple of further exercises, in using active and reflective listening, helpful.

Something for you to try

Active and reflective listening

This opens up the power of using active and reflective listening with your child. Use an egg timer or set a kitchen timer or alarm clock to two minutes. Toss a coin for who goes first. The one going first gets two minutes having the floor, being able to talk without interruptions. Choose whatever you like – at first it may be telling the other person about something that excited or pleased you that day. Later you can use the opportunity to tell them something that worries or hurts you. The task for the other is to use active listening to encourage – making eye contact, nodding and umming and ah-ing to let the other know they are paying full attention. Then, swap over.

When you've had a few goes at active listening, try reflective listening. In this the listener repeats back to the speaker what they've said to check out that they have understood – "So, if I've got this right you're saying . . .".

When you've each had a go talk over the experience. How did it feel to be given a free rein knowing you weren't going to be interrupted? How did it feel to need to listen and make no comment? How did it feel to have to show you understood by reflecting back the other persons' words, and how did it feel to have that done to you? Did you feel you learnt anything, by being listener or speaker?

Being aware of non-verbal communication

Another technique that can help with communication when you do find you are having frequent arguments is to practise what you may be saying with aspects other than your words. Often, people say "But I only said . . . !" and feel aggrieved they might have been taken the wrong way. And as we've already reported, at times a teenager can feel angry simply if her mother coughs! Sometimes however, it's not so much oversensitivity as a reaction to our body language. If you have something to say and suspect it might lead to an argument, stand in front of a mirror and say it, and then think about how you came across. Angry, accusing, judgemental? How would you have responded? How would you prefer to hear what you just said? Try it again, until you feel you'd respond in the way you'd like the other person to react to your request.

How early do we have to make rules about digital use?

From talking to parents we're very clear about this – you need to begin thinking and acting about these matters early. Even if you don't actually hand over the devices, children see you use them from birth. And even if they don't have access at home, many primary schools are now incorporating digital technology into their lessons. By the time you think they are ready, such as the beginning of secondary school or becoming a teenager, children could well have already taken on practices, assumptions and attitudes that may not be helpful.

So you need to begin the conversation and do the training well before it will be put into practice, so that when you do hand over their first phone or allow access to tablet or laptop, you are restating rules already rehearsed. That way, they will remember and act on them and have them ingrained.

It will be important to take the age of the child, and her or his capabilities into account – what is necessary and vital for children alters from year to year, and when it comes to teenagers we have to move from being gatekeeper – protecting, knowing best and refusing access – to being guide and mentor – deliberating, advising and negotiating. But if you don't consider the rules and boundaries early you may end up like one father:

> "He's six and I know is on his computer four hours a day. I know that's not desirable – last week the weather was fabulous and his older sister was out in the garden running around. He was inside with his friends playing games. But if I say no, I get shouts and arguments and it just sometimes doesn't feel worth the fight even though I know I should be tougher."
>
> Elliott, father of 6-year-old son and
> 8-year-old daughter

From birth you need to have a digital strategy, setting an amount of screen time you will allow. The earlier you decide this the easier it is to impose – you simply, matter of factly, say that's the rule in your home. "My friends can . . . ", "My friends say . . . ", "You're being mean!" can be met with the clear, unambiguous and non-confrontational statement "That's fine. In this home this is how we do it." It's never too late to introduce rules and boundaries. You simply say "Yes, it's different now. I realised I had it wrong. Now, in this home this is how we do it."

General household digital rules should be:

- Turn off technology when you get home for a period, and at mealtimes – all of you. No television in the background, no mobile phones or tablets at table.
- Meals to be taken at a table, not from laps in front of screens.
- Watch programmes, not television – in other words, choose specific things to watch rather than just having it on.
- Help children watch with a critical eye – discuss what you see.

- Don't let screens be the only entertainment or source of knowledge in your home – read books and enjoy activities too.
- Allow 'check-in times' to social media in the evening for you all but make it at an agreed time, for a specific time and make sure you have something definite to move on to at that point – family fun time or bedtime routine beginning. The time online or on social media comes out of their agreed limit for the day. Cooperate in keeping a check on all your screen time.

Screen time

There are various opinions on what should be our guidelines for screen use for our children. Screens, don't forget, encompass television, computers, tablets, mobile phones – anything that has a lit screen. The only electronic device that doesn't count is a reader that uses the technology that means the screen is like a sheet of paper. But the consensus seems to be that we should be aiming for:

- 0–2 years of age; never
- 3–5 years of age; no more than one hour a day
- 6–18 years of age; no more than two hours a day

Within that, there should be no programmes or games that contain violence or pornography.

Since children do what you do, not what you say it would be prudent to assign yourselves the same limits. No more than two hours a day. Too little? It's all about prioritising and making choices. Seeing you manage that is a very good example for them. It means you don't have a screen on in the background for the sake of it – you engage with specific programmes/games/projects, not screens.

You might have to stretch that guideline, with your children almost certainly using screens for school work. They may need to use a digital device for homework, or they may come home already having exceeded the guidelines! But keeping that in mind, you may then want to be strict on how much they get to see at home or on weekends.

But let's unpick this because it might seem unrealistic. No screen at all for under 2-year-olds? As quite a few parents told us, they use all sorts of digital devices around their children so it was almost impossible to shield them entirely. And some research seems to suggest hand-eye coordination might be improved with tablet use, and interest certainly piqued. So the key message might be that screens are to be used with discretion and constant monitoring. Don't just plonk a child in front of a screen to keep them quiet. And while – we've all done it – using television or a tablet to keep them from under your feet while doing something that needs doing, make sure you constantly check. Have a conversation about what they're seeing, make sure it remains the right programme, and switch off when it's over. And that in fact applies to all ages, not just to little ones.

Discussing programmes and games

What should you talk about during or after a programme or a game? Try these:

If your child is 2 to 4:

> Tell me what you were doing
> That was a lovely song, let's sing it together
> Who did you see?
> What were they doing?
> Were they happy or sad – why?

If your child is 5 to 8:

> Tell me about the game/story
> Was there something you/the characters had to do? How did you/they work it out?
> Was it about something you'd like to do?
> Who/what are your favourites – why?
> What made the game/programme exciting/scary/funny?

If your child is 9 to 11:

> What happened and what were the consequences?
> Which characters did you like or dislike – why?

Did anything in this game/programme surprise you or
teach you something you didn't know?

Does this game/programme mean to teach you
something or get a certain message across?

If your child is 12 to 18:

Does the situation you saw seem realistic?

Do any of your friends act like that?

What would happen in real life if someone acted that
way?

Do any of these characters seem like 'types'?

Why do so many games/shows repeat the same stories or
create such similar characters?

In reality shows, what do the participants stand to gain
or lose by appearing on the show?

Reality shows often rely on 'jeopardy' – a 'will they/
won't they?' scenario. Do you think this is genuine or
manipulated?

Media literacy

What you are helping children and young people acquire is
the ability to be media literate. That means being able to
discriminate, to be critical and analytic. If you know what
you enjoy and what you do not you can then prioritise –
choose not to watch randomly. Media literacy means you
can recognise what is real and unreal, appropriate and not
appropriate and draw boundaries. It means understanding
much of what you see on a screen can be unreal, fake, air
brushed or manipulated to give you one viewpoint only. By
talking and examining you can help them – and yourself –
to see that you often have to take on all points of view to
see the genuine story. Or ask the question – who benefits
from me believing what I'm being told here? Could there be
a motive for them wanting me to believe one thing rather
than another – what could it be?

Some schools cover these issues, but we would encourage parents to be in partnership dealing with it at home too.
If your child's school does not cover this it would be worthwhile raising the subject with teachers – it is too important

for it not to be discussed in as many spheres of influence in your child's life as possible.

Devices in bedrooms

Which brings us to possibly the most important rule, around digital devices of any sort in bedrooms.

Parents have real challenges on this issue. On the one hand you need to respect and allow for the fact that teenagers, and even younger children, have a need for privacy. They should be able to talk with their friends away from the prying eyes and ears of parents and siblings. They should also have the space for themselves to search for information or places to discuss issues that worry them – about sex, gender, body changes etc. If you give them this leeway they are more likely to come to you when they are ready. When it comes to homework, bedrooms may be the only places in your home where they can get on in either peace or quiet or whatever conditions they find conducive.

What you don't want to allow is for them to slip away into isolation. Left to their own devices a young person may find themselves accessing sites, information and even contact with people that can be harmful. The more you encourage them to be part of the family and to share proximity and entertainment, the more you listen to them and pay attention, the less they may need or have the opportunity to escape.

In early days, insist they only use devices in public spaces. As they get older and have proved reliable and responsible, allow as a privilege for them to spend some time out of their screen allowance in their own rooms with laptops or tablets for homework and devices including mobile phones to be in touch with friends. But continue an open discussion on what they do about it, and why and how.

What you can be adamant about is that there should be no TVs and no games consoles in bedrooms at any time. This allows you to see how much they access and help them keep those screen-time limits, and what they see or take part in. Set an unbreakable rule that mobile phones go off and come out of bedrooms an hour before your children go to sleep.

Explain that while you acknowledge their need and right to respect and privacy you also have to balance this with safeguarding them. When they first start using digital devices make it clear – they have to earn the right to be trusted by showing they can be.

You could have a discussion with each child about what helps and hinders them do homework. We may have the idea that it has to be done in media silence, alone. If we cast our minds back to our own childhood we may find we didn't do it that way, having music or TV on in the background or doing it with friends or siblings. And with some schools, pupils are required and recommended to be in touch with friends as they work, to share ideas and tips. That social media conversation may be about trivialities – it may be part of the project. So talk it through, ask them to be honest and self-aware and negotiate their screen time with that in mind.

Being a role model

Being a role model for your children means you have to keep to the same rules as you set them. No TV in your bedroom either, phones and computers to go off at night. If you love watching TV from bed make it the big treat for holiday time in a hotel, or the present you promise yourself when they leave home! It may be felt by you as too much of a sacrifice but think of this: the hassle involved in only being able to watch TV in your living area can be more than made up by the fact you won't have to get involved in the ongoing and bitter conflict around "You do it, why can't I??" Being a parent is hard and setting a good example can involve difficult choices. It pays off.

What sort of technology might be an asset for your children? Look for devices or games that:

- add a new spin to an old game, but not for the sake of it
- allow children to be creative, to have control over aspects of it
- encourage collaboration and sharing – anything that encourages children to play together, communicate or compete will help promote social development

- allow children with special needs to play too
- encourage children to be physically active as well as use screens

What sort of technology should you avoid or monitor closely? Look out for devices or games that:

- make a game technical or digital when it doesn't need it – a card or board game doesn't have more value and may be less accessible if it's on a screen
- repeat the same moves with little development or give children and young people no opportunity to develop problem solving skills and use their imagination
- are addictive (games that lead you on and make you want to persist are good; games that actually reward you too often and too easily, with no tools for regulating the time you spend on them so you go on pressing the buttons, are bad)
- have or connect to apps and other games that constantly offer paid-for additions or let children and young people access inappropriate material

Routines

When you are looking to establish a set of rules and boundaries around any family issue, including digital use, one important area to explore is that of routines. As you saw with the example of Simon, setting a homecoming routine made an enormous difference to how he and his family began and then enjoyed their evenings together. Routines give you structure and stability and often help you and your family in so many ways. How you all make that transition from your day – work, school, whatever – to being together can make the difference between conflict and harmony.

Suggestions to begin an evening together more constructively may be:

- agreeing a media-free – no electronic devices – half or full hour while everyone has something to eat and chats about the day. Phones off and in the box

- allowing everyone a 'calm-down' period to gather themselves – having a shower, listening to music, relaxing
- everyone having a time slot – one, two, three minutes – to be heard without interruption. This can be to ask a question, tell about a triumph or disaster, ask for help or sympathy, make a complaint

Thinking about the three questions:

What goes wrong?
What are the triggers?
What could we do differently?

. . . you could construct your own homecoming routine.

Three other flash points for conflict that would benefit from a routine might be pre-mealtime, bedtime and mornings.

Key times

We have already outlined a strategy we call How To Get Your Child To Listen To You and Do As You Ask, in Chapter 9, Communication. This can be especially useful when wanting to get your family round the table to eat. Rather than shouting from the kitchen, make the effort to go and speak to them and alert them to the upcoming mealtime. Best of all, using this direct person-to-person connection often results in them coming early to help you prepare a meal. As already discussed, when your children take part in putting a meal together they are far less likely to be fussy about it.

Bedtimes are especially key times when you are trying to establish a digital strategy. Most parents are aware that 4–5-year-olds need 10–12 hours sleep and 7–12-year-olds need 9–10 ½ hours a night. But do we all realise teenagers need 9¼ hours? Light-emitting technology disrupts sleep patterns and makes it hard to get to sleep. You may well be up to speed with the idea of having a bedtime routine for young children. Let's look at what that might involve, and then go on to seeing what components of that can and should be carried over to a routine for older children.

Almost all children will resist the idea of going to bed. They don't want to miss out on what is happening with you. If there are children of different ages in the family, the elders will want to establish their status by staying up later and the youngsters will want to join in. Getting into an argument over bed times only prolongs the misery with everyone getting entrenched.

So the most effective way is:

- Having a plan. Make sure you and your partner have agreed bedtimes and the routine that leads to it. You can be flexible for special occasions but the more you keep to this, the happier you will all be.
- Note that caffeine stays in your body for between 8 and 14 hours and keeps you awake. Most fizzy drinks have the same amount in them as coffee, the 'energy' drinks have two to three times the amount. No caffeine after lunch.
- Your routine begins at least an hour before bedtime. All screens should go off and boisterous play cease when there is an hour to go. Children and teenagers should know this is the time they begin to clear up – tidying away games, saying goodnight to friends on social media, switching off media and wi-fi routers and generally winding down.
- You will factor in meals, hot baths and teeth cleaning around this point depending on their age.
- Send young people to bed, whatever their age, half an hour before they need to go to sleep. That half hour should be spent reading books or devices that have 'paper' technology screens, and talking with you. There is no substitute for reading young children a bedtime story. It gives them the chance for a quiet and consistent time each day to have your undivided attention. Some days they may bring up things that have worried them, or pleased them. Other days they simply value your company, showing them that you value them. Reading books passes on so many important messages, about the joy of learning, the value of imagination and creativity and the significance of shared memories and experiences. In many families, reading bedtime stories continues far beyond childhood into the teenage years for that reason.

"It sounds strange but I read to my sons right up
until the day the eldest went to uni. We read them
the first *Harry Potter* when it first came out and went
on reading the series year after year. It was a race
between our finishing and his going away! They both
say they still miss it – we read stories when they
come home for Christmas!"

Brent, father of sons aged 25 and 26

• If your children feel past the age for being read to, give
  time for a chat then leave them to read for themselves.
  Books or 'paper-like technology' screens only. With children being read to, ten minutes before lights out leave
  them to read for themselves. With whatever age, return
  for a last goodnight kiss before lights out.

Making this an unshakable routine has the effect of putting children and teenagers onto a well-worn course. Since
it all ends with undivided attention and a kiss, rather than
being something to be fought against, it becomes something
to aspire to. It allows you to both set and monitor the time
they settle down and see that they are not breaking rules
on technology in bedrooms, but it does so casting you as the
person caring for them rather than the cop. Kids who have
got to the age when they say kissing and such stuff is silly
or embarrassing will be devastated if you take that at face
value and stop. It's one of the times as a parent you need to
listen to the meaning underneath the words.

Having a bedtime routine for them is helped by your
showing you have one for yourselves too. Wind down to
bedtime by turning off media and going to bed only with
your partner and a good book. Cats allowed too, but no
electronics.

You can sidestep many areas of conflict by having set
routines that avoid trigger points. For mornings it helps
if you've all set out what you need for the day the evening
before, and know you have to arrive at breakfast at an
agreed time. If you make a habit of constantly reminding
and chivvying, you remove from your children the ability to
be responsible for themselves.

"When I did a parent's course one of the issues for me was that mornings were a nightmare and one of my sons would persistently leave his packed lunch behind. I'd have to go to the school on my way to work and leave it for him, and be late. The general consensus was that I should stop doing it all for them. They never had any incentive to change while I covered for them and stopped them experiencing the consequences. I just felt it would reflect on me but the other mums said no, it was their look out. So I told them breakfast was at 7.30, school bus was at 8 and if they were late that was their look out. And no more lunch box runs! They did it once – missed the bus and had to wait until I was ready to go so they got detention. And he went without lunch once. Never again. And no more arguments because I wasn't nagging."

Marie, mother of 12- and 15-year-old sons

For other situations – exam revision, before and after holidays, family events such as Christmas – whether you call it tradition or routine, you need to craft a set way of managing the situation so there is every incentive to follow the well-worn route instead of arguing over what needs to be done or what you expect.

Setting family rules

Rules are best established by 'nudging' people into them rather than imposing them. You do this by:

- Using ideas storming to agree a set of rules that works for the whole family. You put your point of view and they put theirs and you each explain what's important and why. You can get them to sign up to a set of rules and observe boundaries around digital use, and many family issues, if you listen and explain, negotiate and compromise. Some things of course you stick at – no digital technology at the table or in bedrooms at night, for instance. But by giving a little on some issues you can gain a lot on others.

- See setting rules and boundaries not as a conflict or a battle but an opportunity for discussion. Point out to them that this gives them the chance to make their own suggestions and requests.
- Give pleasant alternatives to screen use, rather than just banning them. Offer board games – old fashioned but still surprisingly popular. In good weather, a walk or other activity. Getting fit together can be fun as well as good for you. Cook, bake, discover your family history. Ask them to come up with ideas of what they might like to do as a family. Your children will also value the opportunity to spend time on their own with one parent – a shopping trip or an outing round a particular interest.
- To wean them off wanting to spend all their time on social media, suggest a choice of box sets and films to sit down and watch together. Or use creative gaming to build your own castle, town, community.

Media monitoring

We've talked about the importance of media monitoring – what do we mean by this? It's easy to slide into letting your children – and allowing yourself – behave in certain ways without thinking it through or examining it. So a child watches a TV programme and next week watches that one and the one after. They pick up a tablet and fiddle about with it and next week are not only proficient at a game but also expecting to play it every day. Before you know it you have a 6-year-old spending four hours a day on screens, and prepared to scream the house down if you intervene. Or a teenager who quite seriously will tell a parent she'd rather die than hand her phone over. You should start off by being the parent who sets the rules and sets the pace. As they grow older you collaborate with them to agree sensible limits and boundaries that they will keep themselves, because they see the reason to do so.

So what do you do? The best way of course is to have your plan ready before they begin watching, using or playing.

Have in mind the limits you will impose. When they begin to see screens or use digital technology make a point of doing it with them, supervising, discussing and taking part.

Tell them what time limits you will set and stand firm on them. Give them a choice of how they may spread their screen use, across social media via phone or computer, games console or TV, but maintain the limits.

Discuss flexibility around age and stage. If you have more than one child you are certain to have times when one is old enough to move up to more use and the other will object. Stand firm and explain that's how growing up works – you eventually get to the stage when you have more privileges. And you also can lose them for bad behaviour.

As they get older and go on the internet, be at hand to help them when they join any site – from the children's playsites to later being on social media. Insist you know their passwords and coach them through setting privacy settings. Check those regularly.

"I have access to all of my child's passwords until she reaches adulthood. It's the rule. I do spot checks to make sure she is using it appropriately or it's taken away."

Toni, daughter aged 14

Talk through what they will be doing online, who they will be talking with and how they will behave. Explain you do respect their right to privacy but your job in keeping them safe supersedes this. You reserve the right to check what they are doing. As they prove responsible and trustworthy, thank them and check less. But always reserve the right to do so. Don't feel guilty about checking.

Discuss flexibility around special occasions. If the rule is watch programmes on TV, there may be times when you want to watch more – during the Olympics for instance. This is where you can model the art of prioritising – choose the ones you watch and drop the ones that are less important. Average your hours over a period so you make up for heavy use in one week by not watching at all for some days or weeks after.

Discuss and agree sanctions for breaking rules. These might be less access for a period or more monitoring. Or loss of some treat or privilege in another area.

Discuss and negotiate on age limits set on programmes, films and games. It is not easy to stand firm, as so many young people and some parents do not observe the age limits on these and you will get "But my friends watch/play this!" However, age limits are there for a reason even if you have issues with some of them (there seems to be more leeway on the depiction of violence than sex, for instance . . .). You of course must decide what content you want your sons and daughters to be exposed to and may disagree with the authorities. But it is something you should think about and discuss.

Parents should take an interest, and can set limits. It is possible to say that you as a parent will not allow use of games designed for an age group older than your child or young person. Be ready to say "I don't care if your friends are allowed to do this. In this home my care for you means you will not do it." All games and films show their rating; most of the violent and exciting games, such as *Call of Duty*, *Grand Theft Auto* or *Assassin's Creed*, are 18+. But the most important issue is that if you break rules so will they. Resist pester power but note children will swap games amongst themselves so if left unmonitored may well play inappropriate games. Talk it though with them and explain why you will be keeping to the rules and want them to, as well, and ask other parents what is their stance. Be aware that if they view something that disturbs them and feel they can't confess to you or ask for reassurance or explanation this is far more damaging – reassure them even if they have broken rules they can still come to you.

Setting limits

How do you tell a teenager they can't have technology in their bedroom at certain times or without certain expectations? Or that unlike their friends they won't be given *Call of Grand Assassin's Creed* for Christmas? Or that you won't allow them to join certain social media sites until they are 13, and certainly not if they want to say they are 17? One difficulty seems to be that this generation of parents wants to be friends with their children. Perhaps that's because we are of a generation that wants to be 'liked'. Or maybe we've taken the idea that children should be both seen and heard and respected just that step too far. Another difficulty is that there is a lack of skill, confidence and knowledge. Whatever the reason, many parents find it hard to risk having their children shout "I hate you!" and find it hard to say no or put their foot down. When children say "I hate you!" what they mean is "I'm angry!" – sometimes at you, sometimes at themselves and sometimes at the world. Avoiding having them say it doesn't make such feelings go away – it actually means they never have the chance to manage such emotions.

There is a place for negotiation and compromise. But as parents you have the final say and there are times when you know what you are asking or saying is right, and that's an end of it. How do you tell a teenager? You tell them. Kindly, calmly but firmly. No, we don't have TV in bedrooms in our house. No, you do not have your phone in your room overnight. No, you can't have more screen time tonight. Yes, everything goes off an hour before bed. And you ignore the histrionics and stand firm.

Ask them, would you expect instant results and gratification in the real world, do you get constant reinforcement of success and the chance to try again if you fail as you do online or in games? Do some of the things you see online make you feel certain things are acceptable and 'normal' that perhaps would make you uncomfortable in the real world, or that you wouldn't want said or done to you? Help your children to learn to walk away. If someone pestered them in real life young people may be inclined to be polite, but mostly they'd walk away. Help them see they can do the same online.

Digital detoxes

As well as having limits on screen use per day or per week, families would greatly benefit from having regular digital detoxes.

"It caused howls of protest but we took our lot for a holiday to an area of France where the mobile signal was rubbish. The gite didn't have a TV and we made them leave their tablets and games stuff behind. They sulked for the first day or so. Then they began to realise swimming in the pool, visiting markets and cooking up fabulous meals and sitting outside watching the stars as we ate was pretty cool. When we got back we made Sunday digital no-go day. We go out and do things – some of the things we found were such fun on our holiday."

Stephi, mother of 9-year-old son and 14- and 15-year-old daughters

"My parents insisted we had Sundays switched off and my brother and me were horrified – we said we'd be outcasts next day at school and miss out on all the good jokes and stuff. First couple of times we did things like hide our phones in the bathroom and go up there and check in. They got wise to that and made us hand them in, and switched everything off, then made us go out for bike rides and stuff. Weird thing was that after a few weeks we got used to it. We didn't miss out on as much as I thought – it was all stuff that didn't matter anyway. So now, we kind of like it. I tell my friends they should try it and a couple have."

Isabella, 17

Choose a holiday or weekend or just a daytrip destination that is off grid, or do it yourself by turning off all technology and leaving it off, or leaving it behind. As with any detox, you'll all feel dreadful at first – anxious, jumpy and touchy. Soon you'll find it restful. And you don't miss out on as much as you thought, which is telling.

Detox rules

- Keep busy – it's when you are bored that the pull of social media or other digital use becomes irresistible.
- Ask everyone to note when you thought about and wanted to reach for a device – mark these as triggers and act to avoid them or be prepared to resist when they repeat.
- Agree set times to detox – one day a week, at least one holiday a year.
- Discuss what it felt like at first to detox – and how it feels after a few times

Discuss with them the issues of digital footprint – the trail, traces or 'footprints' that people leave online. Explain that rather than being free, most of what we get from the internet is 'paid for' with information, about ourselves. iRights are being discussed at present, to afford every child and young person the rights to:

- edit or delete any content they have created
- know who is holding or profiting from their information
- be protected from illegal practices and supported if confronted by upsetting content

The problem is that at present these rights are not set in place. It's up to us to help our children protect themselves and ask for help when they need it.

How it affects them

Young people may make bad choices about digital use. They may get into the habit of constant use or take risks with disclosing information. Or make nasty comments online without thinking through how this may feel. This won't be because they are unpleasant or stupid or can't foresee the consequences but because the teenage brain rewards risky behaviour with a jolt of dopamine. Teenagers seek sensation, whether through fast driving, fighting, arguing, substance abuse or trolling online. And they may ignore your warnings because they so want to both push boundaries and assert their independence. For tweens and teenagers, their friends matter as much as you do, so you have to both understand and negotiate to help them keep safe. One way is offering other, better, safer ways of getting the buzz – sports, adventure, achievements.

Talk with your children about priorities. Not being part of the cool gang perhaps but having friends who value them and whom they value. Not being popular but feeling good about themselves – people tend to like people who like themselves. Discuss body image – and be very careful how you discuss it and describe yourselves as adults. Worry about being fat? So will they. Make snide comments about people? So will they.

Teenagers particularly, but some younger children too, have used the possibilities of digital technology to become wrapped up in posting 'selfies' – pictures of themselves. Some of this is entirely benign. We would have done it if we'd had the technology – instead, we used to cram into photo booths to take pics of ourselves with best friends. They do it because adolescence is the age during which how you look and present yourselves is so important. I see me therefore I am . . . Rather than criticise, empathise and share how you did it too. But use it to initiate conversations about body image. Are the shots they see of their role models realistic? What do you have to do to achieve a body like that? Unhealthy dieting? An exercise routine you could only manage if you didn't have to fit in school or daily employment? Digitally manipulated pictures?

Raise their self-confidence and self-esteem

The better young people feel about themselves the less importance they may place on constant external affirmation of the sort offered by social media. And of course, the more involved and engaged you are and thus they are with other aspects of family life, the less they need to reach for a device to entertain them.

Help them raise self-confidence and esteem by:

- Prioritising family meal times – the more you just chat with them, welcome them, enjoy their company and spend time with them, the better they feel about themselves and you.

- Compliment them regularly. Do frequent 'drive-bys' – toss a "You look nice", "Thank you for doing that", "So nice to spend time with you!" in passing.
- Step back and get them to practise skills. With small children, ask them to carry that full glass of water to the table. Have a cloth ready for spills but make no fuss – they can't learn if you don't respect the struggle. As they get older, ask them to go to the shop, call friends to fix an outing themselves, make bookings, shop for and cook a meal.
- Get them to do a 'Maya Van Wagenen': the American teenager spent a month copying the advice in a 1950s etiquette handbook – being polite to all and smiling and making friends with each gang of friends at school. Despite many rebuffs, within weeks she was shocked to discover she had gone from being bullied to being viewed as popular.
- Enrol them in team sports and activities such as The Duke of Edinburgh Award Scheme. If their schools don't support such initiatives, ask them why not? And look to local youth organisations such as guides or scouts that will do so. To help young people regulate moods and achieve self-control and promote determination, perseverance, and self-regulation look at ways you and your entire family can look after yourselves. Regular physical exercise – playing team games, going to a gym, walking, running, cycling, swimming – and mind/body exercises like tae kwon do all help you build self-esteem and self-control along with helping you get and stay healthy. Doing them together promotes family bonds.
- Make doing chores mandatory. If your child does their share round the house it encourages several things. One is a sense of ownership – it's their home and they have a pride in being a contributing member of the family. It prepares them for their future when they will have to manage. It helps them respect what it takes to run a home and family, and thus to understand and respect you.

- Change the money you give them from pocket money to an allowance. You give them more, but with the responsibility of being in charge of certain expenditure – discuss with them what. And once started, don't bail them out. If they blow the entire month or quarter's allowance in one and then are stuck, that's a really valuable lesson you'd ruin if you gave in.
- After 13, suggest they get a job for extra spending money or savings.
- Let them be bored occasionally. One of the unexpectedly destructive aspects of being constantly 'on' is that children never need get bored – they just reach for social media or entertainment. Which means they have less incentive to be innovative, determined, intellectually curious. They don't have to go look for something to do, make, read. Part of insisting on time out from being always digitally connected is to allow and encourage them to seek other ways to be engaged and fulfilled. Go read a book, ride a bike, climb a tree, make a card or craft something, bake a cake, sing a song, dance, run, dream . . .
- Don't try to learn their slang. This is partly because it develops and evolves so fast you'll be out of date and there is nothing quite as tragic as on oldie trying to be 'kewl'. But mainly it's because slang is there for a reason. We used it and every generation does, to make a statement about autonomy and separateness and to draw a boundary between 'me' and 'you'. For tweens and teens, that's healthy. It shows crass lack of respect to trespass.

Communication and engagement

It is vital that parents remain engaged. This does not mean you sitting next to the child all the time, but it does mean being aware of what is happening, showing care and concern, and working with the child or young person to help them develop the skills so that they can keep themselves safe off- and online. So what do we do about the issues we found were the real threats to our children online? Issues such as dealing with conflict, friendship, cyberbullying, posting and uploading something you might regret, harmful content, sex and rites of passage? Here are some ideas.

Conflict – keeping arguments real

Young people have always had spats with friends and family. Emotional bonds tend to be felt so much more strongly by young people and these arguments have the power to linger and cause pain for ages. Or, indeed, be forgotten the next moment. But in the throes of the moment, young people today can reach for the internet. Whether the argument is with you, their friends or someone else's argument half a world away that they can be drawn into, putting it online can entirely change the situation.

In the old days, if we'd been given a dressing down by our parents we'd have retreated (or been sent) to our rooms where we might have meditated on our failings and possibly repented. Even if we'd still felt hard done by, at least we'd have to emerge and fall into some sort of line. Today a reprimanded teenager can retreat to their room and upload to the internet a rant, a video and possibly even proof recorded on a hidden phone of your unwarranted attack on their rights and dignity. There it might gain widespread support from friends and other teenagers not only on their own network but possibly across the world and amongst strangers. Some parents have been so traumatised by the abuse directed their way by this that they hesitate now to dispute with their children. And arguments with friends can 'go viral' too, as they upload the argument and appeal for support, or join in someone else's appeal.

It's a challenge to manage this. What we do need to get our kids to understand is that an online argument through social media, or by creating special websites, is a totally different order of things than shouting and slammed doors, or the passing of notes or mouth-to-mouth rumours around school or a neighbourhood. Real-world interaction may linger but can be forgotten and smoothed over, by the protagonists either letting it go or making up. Putting it online gives it a far greater audience of people who may not be personally involved and so could be keen to exploit or encourage more conflict, not resolution. It becomes arms' length entertainment, not real people with real feelings. However much you change your mind in the real world, what you have said remains online. Forever. It goes on hurting, and goes on making you all look terrible. Keep arguments real, we have to tell them.

This means we need to model good behaviour. Do not shame your child, and help them to see shaming can hurt – a lot – and come back to bite you. One UK mother, for instance, decided to film her 8-year-old son stumbling through and trying to make sense of a letter he had received apparently sent by Santa, telling him he was on the naughty list and had 13 days to show he deserved his presents. His tears and distress, and that of his 4-year-old sister, was uploaded by her to YouTube, where it remains. If it means you set boundaries and rules with a little more skill and assertiveness rather than losing it, all the better. Check twice, send once, and always count to ten.

Friendship

Teaching a generation of children used to looking down at a screen to look up when they interact with others and make eye contact, to smile, maybe even to kiss or shake hands is a challenge! French teenagers do it – watch a group of young people meet up in a French cafe and each newcomer is greeted separately by everyone with a hug and kiss (how many kisses, from two to four, dictated by where you are in France) or a handshake. French teenagers talk amongst themselves, only occasionally looking at a handset, and they then tend to show those around them what has been posted. In contrast, British teenagers seem to drift up and join the group, sometimes only being acknowledged by their immediate neighbours but certainly with no formal welcome. Many then sit communing more with their devices than those around them. It might be interesting and helpful to ask your children what they think – what they like or don't like about the way they meet together and whether they might want to change the behaviour in their own social group. It only takes one to try something new to have it catch on, you can suggest.

Ask young people to watch out for one another and accept that self-harm, anorexia, suicide are not glamorous or admirable. One worrying aspect of social media is the fashion for posting marvellously loving, caring and affirmative messages on someone's blog after they have died; the belief seems to be that the person can hear them, that dying is somehow temporary and not real. We need to get ourselves and our young people to recognise the need to say nice things while the person is alive, to recognise the warning signs and reach for help.

Leaning in

Cyberbullying and pornography, access to harmful content, the possibility of being groomed, and the temptation for a digitally skilled young person – a 'geek' – to show off their expertise by hacking are perhaps the most worrying aspects of internet use. Can you protect them – and, if so, how? As we've already said, by leaning in. By being engaged.

Cyberbullying

We've talked about how easy it seems for cyberbullying to happen, and the astounding power and reach of such behaviour. What seems to facilitate it happening is the disconnect between what people say on the internet and particularly on social media and what they might say or do when face-to-face with the other person. The screen makes it unreal. The screen means the people joining in with the unkind behaviour can tell themselves it isn't serious, it's only a joke, it's just banter. Shown hurtful messages and invited to rethink how it might feel to receive such a message, the majority of young people will refrain.

We need to ask our children to be kind. To never, ever post anything they wouldn't say to someone face-to-face, or would not be happy to have someone say to you. Talk it through with them. Ask them to ask themselves, before posting something 'clever', "What would a grandmother the other side of the world think of this? And – what would MY grandmother think of this?" You could even suggest the consequence for violating this simple rule would be . . . to show it to granny and see what she does.

If your child is involved don't let it go on. If they are the target, help them block and ignore hurtful messages and people, and talk it through so they see they aren't to be taken seriously. But also, we need to help them grow a thicker skin. Abuse always feels so personal and targeted. Even when it is addressed to a specific person, it never is really about them. People are unkind and abusive because of something to do with them. They're having a hard time, someone has made them feel bad and they're trying to get back a feeling of power and control. Or, it's simply a game and they don't realise the real effect.

You can demand the social media site remove the messages. All now have a 'report' button you can click on to alert them to anything offensive. In some cases the Internet Service Provider of the perpetrators would remove their access. You can contact the school, and ask them to use their bullying policy to act. If the school doesn't respond appropriately, you can ask the school governors or the local authority to do so. And of course you can contact the local police. Save and retain all messages – they are evidence.

If it's your child taking part, however small a part, you can do two things. You can find out why they felt this was either needful or acceptable, and deal with that. And you can make it clear that, whatever the reason, their behaviour is unacceptable and have them apologise and offer reparation.

Sex

Young people turn to the internet to find out about sex for one reason. That is, they are normally, naturally curious about the subject and we don't address that. Personal, social and health education is appalling in this country. And because it has been for so long, most parents find the subject a difficult one to address so can't help. Before the internet we looked for answers in books, 'topshelf' magazines and 'blue' movies. Now, they reach for the internet and get far more than they bargained for. Pornography might be fine if what they saw depicted was mutual, healthy relationships. What they often get is abusive and violent sex. To counter the normalisation of unhealthy images that young people are getting from pornography online, there are good programmes and projects available in some schools. The Everyday Sexism Project encourages girls to speak out about the behaviour around them and multiplatform campaigns try to inform young people about consent and what constitutes sexual assault. More and more young people of both sexes are beginning to recognise the sort of behaviour they see in pornography is not what they want or what they want to be. But it needs parents to speak out and demand better from schools. And to inform themselves and become more relaxed at offering the chance to discuss sexual matters at home too. Charities such as Family Lives (see appendix) offer support both to parents and young people, and schools, on this issue. The PSHE Association is the national body for Personal, Social, Health and Economic Education. It supports professionals and campaigns for better PSHE in schools. (see appendix) and can help you ask your children's school to offer more help.

Sexting

We need to ask our young people to think twice if not 20 times about sending sexts. They often feel it is an intimate picture between them and a selected person but the chances of it going round their friends, the school, the internet are high. Suggest your young person downloads the app Zipit from Childline. It contains all sort of advice and witty comebacks when asked to sext – such as a graphic to send to someone asking for a nudie pic that is a flying pig with the line "Never. Gonna. Happen". Part of our job is to help them grow a resilience that allows them to cope with whatever they encounter, on- or offline. What is necessary is to help all of us recognise if we wouldn't do it offline – strip off naked on the bus because the friend or stranger asked you to, or tell someone to their face you thought they were ugly and should kill themselves – then you shouldn't do it thinking you're sheltered by the relative anonymity of it being virtual.

Dangerous sites on the internet

Of course a savvy young person can access some forbidden area while in the living room and under your eyes – they simply have an innocent screen on hand to tap up in place of the screen they want to hide when the parent comes near. But it's not easy to maintain secrecy like that, and the fact that you take an interest removes the main reason young people seek destructive areas, because there is something going wrong in their lives and their parents are not paying attention. Teenagers rebel. Teenagers want to flout your rules and push your boundaries – that's a natural part of adolescence. But if they feel loved, listened to, respected and cherished they are highly unlikely to go totally off the rails. As one teenager said to the family-support charity Family Lives:

> "Love your teenager even when they least deserve it.
> Never let their self-esteem drop at home as well as outside.
> Having a good open relationship, I think honesty is key
> so it doesn't matter what the issue so long as everyone
> is honest and open with no judgement and complete
> understanding. Second thing is trust. Parents need to have
> a trustworthy relationship with their teens. If you can't
> give them freedom they can never prove their maturity."

Top tips

- Communication is the key.
- The screen is not the danger; it is the way it is used.
- Your behaviour, as a parent, makes a difference.
- Think about your credibility. Do your teenagers respect what you say?
- Teenagers have needs that are different from the needs of children.
- Have rules and boundaries, which, as with any rules, should be flexible and responsive and change as children get older. And are best created by parent and child together.

Rites of passage

A final strategy you might like to consider in helping your children manage the complexities of digital technology, and the myriad difficulties of growing up, is to consider Rites of Passage.

A rite of passage is a ceremony and marks the transition from one phase of life to another. In some cultures, there are specific celebrations that say to a young person "You are now an adult, no longer a child". In many Western societies, we have no such formal occasion. Which is why young people often make up their own ways of trying to make the point "I'm no longer a child and you're not the boss of me!" Coupled with the drive towards excitement and sensation and the inability to assess risk, it leads to often ill-advised or even dangerous behaviour. If we want to keep our young people safe on digital technology one way would be to acknowledge the natural, normal and common drive amongst adolescents to push boundaries and allow for it. The more we give them responsibility, the less they have to strive for it. The more we encourage them to find safe ways of making this point, the less they need to lean towards the risky and unwise. If we want – and we should want – to say "No, you can't do that now" we should be saying "But you can do this – and at this time you can do that."

There is a world of opportunity out there in the digital world and we want our children to use it and enjoy it. Think of it as that bicycle – something that can get them wonderful places and help them be fit and healthy. But not a good thing to ride on the motorway or reel about on without observing other traffic and highway rules. Hop on wheels yourself, and help each other be safe and be happy.

So, a final . . .

Something for you to try

We've asked you to ideas storm rules with your children for safe internet use. Now, ideas storm how and when to mark their growing up. What will you allow them to access and do now and what else, when? How can you come to an agreement and how can all of you negotiate and comprise? What rite of passage would they appreciate, and what would you like to offer them?

Appendix

More help, support and information

For family or relationship problems your own GP may offer counselling, themselves or from a counsellor in the surgery or through referral.

All social media sites offer advice on their privacy settings and how to apply them, and their rules and what to do if someone is breaking them – such as by sending offensive messages. You just have to look for the information – it's always to be found, by clicking on an icon in each message or on the top of each page.

Family Lives

The national charity that offers help and support in all aspects of family lives and relationships. Website with information and advice and access to Parentchannel.tv with helpful videos, forums, helpline, live chat with help and advice for parents and young people. Face-to-face support groups and workshops and online parenting courses. Extended support for complex difficult issues.

www.familylives.org.uk
Helpline is free, 24/7, even on mobiles: 0808 800 2222

Young Minds

This charity is concerned about the importance of children's mental health; the importance of recognising when a child is troubled and providing adequate support for these children before their problems escalate out of control. They provide a helpline and information for parents and young people.

www.youngminds.org.uk
Helpline: 0808 802 5544

Urban Dictionary

An online dictionary constantly updated and defined by users. It's probably the only way of keeping some check on what on earth your teenagers are talking about!

www.urbandictionary.com

The Site

The Site is a website for young people with information about a wide range of local services, as well as discussion forums and advice such as on moving out.

www.thesite.org

Education City

Provides educational games and activities to families and primary schools to aid learning.

www.educationcity.com

PSHE Association

The national body for Personal, Social, Health and Economic education professionals. Providing members with support, resources, training and guidance but importantly for parents' campaigns for better PSHE provision in schools.

www.pshe-association.org.uk

Doodle

An online scheduling tool that helps you and your family, and friends, agree on times and dates for a meeting.

www.doodle.com

Bullying UK

Part of Family Lives, the national charity that offers help and support in all aspects of family lives. Website with information and advice and access to a helpline, live chat with help and advice for parents and young people. Helpline is free even on mobiles.

www.bullying.co.uk.
Helpline: 0808 800 2222
email: help@bullying.co.uk

Place2Be

Place2Be works in schools providing early intervention mental health support with counselling and other services to young people and their families, when and where they need it most.

www.place2be.org.uk

Beat (formerly the Eating Disorders Association)

The charity that provides information, advice and support on eating disorders such as anorexia, bulimia and binge eating.

www.b-eat.co.uk
email: help@b-eat.co.uk
Helpline: 0345 634 1414
Youthline: 0345 634 7650

PAPYRUS (Parents' Association for the Prevention of Young Suicide)

Provides information and advice for parents, teachers and healthcare professionals. Aims to raise awareness of young suicide, and many members are parents who have lost a child to suicide. They produce a range of publications and materials.

www.papyrus.org.uk
Helpline: 0800 068 41 41

Brook

A charity that provides free and confidential help on contraception and abortion to under 25s.

www.brook.org.uk

Talk to Frank

Provides free and confidential information and advice about drugs. Also has a 24-hour helpline.

www.talktofrank.com
email: frank@talktofrank.com
Helpline: 0300 123 6600
SMS 82111

Internet Matters

Internet Matters is a not-for-profit organisation working with online safety experts to bring you all the information you need to keep your children safe online. They cover issues such as cyberbullying, online grooming, inappropriate content, pornography, self-harm, and more.

www.internetmatters.org

Relate

Offers relationship counselling and life-skills courses through local Relate centres for couples, individuals and young people. Counselling is also available over the telephone, or through the website.

www.relate.org.uk
Tel: 0300 100 1234

British Association for Counselling and Psychotherapy

The association can suggest a counsellor in your area online at their website or via post.

British Association for Counselling and Psychotherapy
BACP House, 15 St John's Business Park, Lutterworth,
Leicestershire LE17 4HB
www.bacp.co.uk

The Institute of Family Therapy

The institute helps with family problems. Write to:

24–32 Stephenson Way, London NW1 2HX.
www.instituteoffamilytherapy.org.uk
Tel: 020 7391 9150

Citizens' Advice Bureau

An independent organisation providing free, confidential
and impartial advice on all subjects to anyone. The address
and telephone number of your local CAB can be found in
the telephone directory or on their site. There is also online
advice on their website.

www.citizensadvice.org.uk

Family Mediators Association

Can put you in touch with trained mediators who work both
with parents and children.

www.thefma.co.uk

National Family Mediation

An umbrella organisation for local family mediation services
and which can provide details of local services in the UK.

www.nfm.org.uk
0300 4000 636

Care for the Family

Care for the Family is a national charity that aims to promote
strong family life and to help those who face family difficulties. They provide parenting, relationship and bereavement

support through events, resources, courses, training and volunteer networks. Their work is motivated by Christian compassion, with resources and support available to everyone, of any faith or none.

www.careforthefamily.org.uk/

Cruse Bereavement Care

Promotes the well-being of bereaved people and enables anyone bereaved by death to understand their grief and cope with their loss. The organisation provides counselling and support, information, advice, education and training services.

www.crusebereavementcare.org.uk
Helpline: 0844 477 9400

The Samaritans

The Samaritans are available 24 hours a day to listen to people in distress and to provide emotional support.

www.samaritans.org
email: jo@samaritans.org
Helpline: 116 123

Mumsnet

Offers a supportive community for parents on the web where you can meet mums in your area and further afield, and find out about local activities.

www.mumsnet.com

Netmums

Offers a supportive community for parents on the web where you can meet mums in your area and further afield, and find out about local activities.

www.netmums.com

Grandparents' Association

The Grandparents' Association supports grandparents whose grandchildren are out of contact with them or who have childcare responsibilities for their grandchildren.

www.grandparents-association.org.uk
Helpline: 0845 4349585

Grandparents Plus

Grandparents Plus provides information about research, resources and support for grandparents and those working with grandparents.

www.grandparentsplus.org.uk
Tel: 0300 123 7015

Release

Release helps parents when their teenage child has been arrested or cautioned by the police for possession of a drug. They also provide support and legal advice about drug-related issues.

www.release.org.uk
email: ask@release.org.uk
Helpline: 020 7324 2989

Al-Anon

Helps anyone who has a friend or family member with a drinking problem – **Alateen** is a section of AL-Anon there especially for the children of problem drinkers.

www.al-anonuk.org.uk
Helpline: 020 7403 0888

ADFAM

ADFAM works with family members facing problems with drugs or alcohol, to help them gain access to a range of specialised services.

www.adfam.org.uk

Families Need Fathers

A registered charity providing information and support on shared parenting issues arising from family breakdown to divorced and separated parents. Support is provided through a national helpline, a website, a network of volunteers, and regular group meetings, held in a variety of locations.

www.fnf.org.uk
24/7 Helpline: 0300 0300 363

The Fatherhood Institute

A think-tank on fatherhood. It offers publications to support fathers and their families.

www.fatherhoodinstitute.org

Separated Dads

A website containing articles and advice for dads living away from their children.

www.separateddads.co.uk/

Families and Friends of Lesbians and Gays (FFLAG)

Provides information and support for parents of lesbian, gay and bisexual young people and their families. They also have local parent support groups, a newsletter, publications and a helpline.

www.fflag.org.uk
email: info@fflag.org.uk
Helpline: 0845 652 0311

Lesbian and Gay Switchboard

LGS provides advice and support for lesbian and gay people, and parents.

www.llgs.org.uk
Helpline: 0300 330 0630

Gingerbread

Provide a helpline with free information to lone parents on issues including benefits, tax, legal rights, family law and contact issues, child maintenance and returning to work. They are able to connect lone parents with other organisations and local groups.

www.gingerbread.org.uk
Free Helpline, on mobiles too: 0808 802 0925

National Association of Child Contact Centres

Promotes safe child contact within a national network of child contact centres. A child contact centre is a safe place where children of separated families can spend time with one or both parents and sometimes other family members. Details of local centres can be found on their website or by ringing them.

www.naccc.org.uk
Tel: 0845 4500 280

CAFCASS (Children and Family Court Advisory and Support Service)

Looks after the interests of children and young people involved in cases in the family courts, ensuring their voices are heard. It helps families to reach agreement over arrangements for their children. CAFCASS only works with families on referral from the court but their website contains useful information, case studies, advice and contact links.

www.cafcass.gov.uk
Tel: 0300 456 4000

Parenting Plans

Putting your children first, a guide for separating parents, is a very helpful booklet, which acts as an outline for your discussions and agreement. Parent plans help you to think of all the things you will need to manage as parents living apart. It's a booklet of questions that you could use to trigger discussion on issues such as day-to-day arrangements, holidays, health, money, and a section to guide you through what to do if you're finding it hard to agree. You can download this from: www.cafcass.gov.uk/grown-ups/parenting-plan.aspx

Resolution – First for Family Law (the Solicitors Family Law Association)

Can give advice on any family dispute and with separation, divorce and new families, and encourage mediation and agreement rather than confrontation.

www.resolution.org.uk

Coram Children's Legal Centre

Offers information on all aspects of child law in England and Wales, particularly contact, parental responsibility and residence orders.

www.childrenslegalcentre.com

NSPCC

The NSPCC can help with advice on keeping your or any other child safe.

www.nspcc.org.uk
Helpline: 0808 800 5000

ChildLine (now part of the NSPCC)

Offers a free confidential helpline to children at risk, open 24 hours.

www.childline.org.uk or www.nspcc.org.uk
Freephone: 0800 1111

The Child Exploitation and Online Protection (CEOP)

The centre works across the UK and abroad to tackle child sex abuse wherever and whenever it happens. Part of their strategy for achieving this is by providing internet safety advice for parents and carers and offering a 'virtual police station' for reporting abuse on the internet.

www.ceop.police.uk

Further reading

How To Have A Happy Family Life, by Suzie Hayman, pub by Teach Yourself General

Raise a Happy Teenager, by Suzie Hayman, pub by Teach Yourself General

Why Won't My Teenager Talk To Me?, by Dr John Coleman, pub by Routledge

How To Talk So Kids Will Listen and Listen So Kids Will Talk, by Adele Faber and Elaine Mazlish, pub by Piccadilly Press

Blame My Brain: the Amazing Teenage Brain Revealed, by Nicola Morgan, pub by Walker

Index